WELCOME

Welcome to Ancient Greece. Western civilization and culture find their deepest roots within the story of the Greek experience. It is one that spans centuries of human existence, of triumph and tragedy, war and peace, discovery and devastation. From it sprang the ideals of Western thought and modern existence.

Famed poet Percy Bysshe Shelley wrote, "We are all Greeks. Our laws, our literature, our religion, our art have their root in Greece."

Such a statement is indeed difficult to disprove. Consider the influence of the Greek way. From the beginning of mankind's expansive exploration of the world – the earth beneath his feet, the seas that stretch to the horizon, and the limitless sky above, the search for timeless truth and understanding began with the Greek civilizations that emerged in the wake of the Bronze Age some three millennia ago.

Then contemplate the mysteries of life, existence, human interaction, the hidden principles of the mind, body, and spirit. These have been discussed and debated early in the shadow of the Acropolis, the agora, and the Aeropagus of ancient Athens. The concepts of honour and duty, devotion to justice, and the defence of home and hearth were nurtured in the spirit of Sparta. As the city states flourished, so the concepts that define the Western perspective were to emerge amid a discourse that profoundly changed the path of human existence and cultural development.

The titans of Western thought, Socrates, Plato, Aristotle; the beginnings of the written historical record, Homer, Herodotus, Thucydides; the progenitors of mathematics and medicine, Hippocrates and Archimedes; the authors of the dramatic tragedy, Sophocles, Euripides, and Aeschylus, each of these and so many more of their forefathers and contemporaries shaped the course of cultural development across the centuries.

Perhaps it is not such a stretch to say that virtually no aspect of the human experience within the Western context exists today solely and exclusively without the touch of the Ancient Greek civilization. The foundations of moral, ethical, and civic conduct were crafted in the eastern Mediterranean cradle. The ideals of beauty, truth, and devotion to duty transcended thought and became tangible elements of existence.

The concept of democracy, rule by the people, saw its embryonic experiment occur in the political lives of Athenians while the basic elements of the law and of civil conduct, crime and punishment, spiritual awakening and the worship of a pantheon of gods provide the modern explorer with a cultural kaleidoscope of adventure and discovery.

From the summit of Mount Olympus, the mythical and mystic home of the gods, to the far reaches of the known world, to the epic of the Trojan War and the timeless works that chronicle its captivating amalgamation of myth and legend, the life and legacy of Ancient Greece are ever reflected in the modern experience. The first Olympic Games occurred there, and the curtain was raised on the theatre as we know it today. Great works of art, architecture, and literature remain to serve as sentinels of the past, a potion for present-day appreciation, and road signs for the fertile contemplation of what may lie in the future.

Ever alive, yet veiled in the mists of the past, Ancient Greece conjures the spirit of adventure, the quest for knowledge and the fullness of human existence. Come and experience the majesty of one of history's grandest civilizations.

Michael E. Haskew
Editor

The ruins of the Parthenon crown the Acropolis in the ancient city of Athens, Greece. (Creative Commons Phanatic via Wikipedia)

CONTENTS

ABOVE: This 18th century painting depicts the mythological figures Jason and Medea. (Public Domain)

ABOVE: The sun god Apollo visits the nine muses who reside at the foot of Mount Olympus. (Public Domain)

ABOVE: The Persian King Xerxes invaded Greece but came to grief after the defeat at the naval battle of Salamis. (Public Domain)

ABOVE: This colourful fresco adorned a tomb of the late 4th century BC unearthed in ancient Macedonia. (Public Domain)

ABOVE: This 19th century painting depicts the death of the Greek mathematician Archimedes at the hands of a Roman soldier in Syracuse. (Public Domain)

ABOVE: Alexander the Great meets King Porus after defeating him in battle. The two later became allies. (Public Domain)

ISBN: 978 1 80282 787 3
Editor: Michael Haskew
Senior editor: Paul Sander
Senior editor, specials: Roger Mortimer
Email: roger.mortimer@keypublishing.com
Cover design: Steve Donovan
Design: SJmagic DESIGN SERVICES, India
Advertising Sales Manager: Brodie Baxter
Email: brodie.baxter@keypublishing.com
Tel: 01780 755131
Advertising Production: Debi McGowan
Email: debi.mcgowan@keypublishing.com

SUBSCRIPTION/MAIL ORDER
Key Publishing Ltd, PO Box 300, Stamford, Lincs, PE9 1NA
Tel: 01780 480404
Subscriptions email: subs@keypublishing.com

Mail Order email: orders@keypublishing.com
Website: www.keypublishing.com/shop

PUBLISHING
Group CEO and Publisher: Adrian Cox
Published by
Key Publishing Ltd, PO Box 100, Stamford, Lincs, PE9 1XQ
Tel: 01780 755131 **Website:** www.keypublishing.com

PRINTING
Precision Colour Printing Ltd, Haldane, Halesfield 1, Telford, Shropshire. TF7 4QQ

DISTRIBUTION
Seymour Distribution Ltd, 2 Poultry Avenue, London, EC1A 9PU
Enquiries Line: 02074 294000.

ORIGINS

The ruins of walls remain at the town of Poliochne on the island of Lemnos. (Creative Commons ale3andro via Wikipedia)

The end of the Neolithic Period, the last of the Stone Age, dates to approximately 3200 BC in southeastern Europe. Even prior to that time, some scholars date the emergence of civilizations that later gave rise to Ancient Greece. During the period, the development of agriculture, raising livestock, widespread use of simple tools, and an appreciation of art were milestones of the communities to come on the Peloponnesian and Attic peninsulas. The transition from the late Neolithic Period to the later Minoan and Mycenaean occurred across at least five centuries. Archaeological discoveries indicate that widespread settlement took root as early as 7000 BC.

The earliest evidence of settlement in the region that encompassed ancient Greece has been traced to the Paleolithic era from 11000 to 3000 BC. The archaeological record has established that the earliest known viable town in Europe was established at Poliochni on the Greek island of Lemnos, which dates to approximately 2500 BC. Greece was a logical destination for migrants from the east and from central Europe. The lure of arable land, the natural beauty of the surroundings, and access to the resources of the sea contributed to the movement of peoples during the period.

Excavations at Poliochni reveal an influence of Anatolia, modern Turkey and the region of Asia Minor, as homes were located closely together and burial sites included figurines of women and animals. The town itself is believed to have predated Troy, which became its chief rival and probably eclipsed Poliochni by the beginning of the second millennium BC.

Despite some of its geographic challenges, high mountains and deep valleys that tended to separate settlements, they were established and thrived in the hospitable climate of the eastern Mediterranean basin. In time, more migrants reached the region, and trade and commerce began to develop. At the same time, elements of civilization began to coalesce, including social classes, aspects of religion, and common language. During the second millennium BC, scholars have identified at least three waves of Indo-European migration into the area of ancient Greece.

Historians of the successive periods in ancient Greek history referred to their predecessors as Pelasgians, a term that has come to describe early residents of the region surrounding the Aegean Sea. Homer wrote that Pelasgians participated in the Trojan War on the sides of both the Greeks and the Trojans. In fact, the archaeological record of Athens and other areas of the Attic peninsula has yielded remnants of settlements that may be described as pre-Greek, including the remains of domesticated animals, tools, pottery, and homes.

Therefore, though relatively little is known of the Pelasgians, some scholars describe the Athenians and others as their descendants. Pelasgian enclaves are believed to have survived into the Classical period, enduring beyond the decline of Mycenaean Greece and the rise of Hellenistic culture. The dawn of the Bronze Age brought with it the development of the Minoan and Mycenaean civilizations that preceded the Dark Age of Greek history.

Even today, research and discovery related to the earliest inhabitants of ancient Greece are ongoing. A single finding often leads to an array of new questions and possible conclusions.

ABOVE: This clay vase dates to the Neolithic period of ancient Greece as early as 5300 BC. (Creative Commons Gary Todd via Wikipedia)

ABOVE: This terra cotta pig was fashioned around 2500 BC in the town of Poliochne. It now resides in the National Archaeological Museum, Athens. (Creative Commons Zde via Wikipedia)

MINOAN AND MYCENAEAN INFLUENCE

The world of ancient Greece began to take form and shape with the confluence of two Bronze Age peoples. The Minoans inhabited the island of Crete in the south along with other spits of land scattered across the Aegean Sea. From the north, the Mycenaeans later ventured into mainland Greece, and in time the two civilizations came together, probably through both conquest and absorption. With the subsequent blending, they formed the foundation of the ancient Greece that is so familiar in Western culture.

The Minoans derive their modern name from Minos, the mythological king of Crete. Little was known of their civilization until the early 20th century, when archaeological excavations conducted by an Englishman, Sir Arthur Francis Evans, revealed the remnants of a tremendous palace at Knossos, an ancient city near present-day Heraklion. The discoveries of Evans and his team were astounding. They uncovered the remains of a thriving, cultured civilization that was contemporary with the Old Kingdom of Ancient Egypt and the early peoples of Mesopotamia, the so-called "Cradle of Civilization."

It is likely that the first Minoans established residence in Crete around 3000 BC, arriving from Asia Minor, an area known in ancient times as Anatolia. They were accomplished seafarers and settled the Greek Isles, principally Crete, from where they traded regularly with partners as far west as the Iberian peninsula and along the coast of North Africa. Renowned as artisans, the Minoans left behind exquisite works wrought in gold, ivory, tin, and faience. They traded for these precious commodities, exchanging olive oil, wine, artwork and jewellery.

The Minoans are believed to have appreciated beauty and natural wonder quite fully. Their paintings, some as brilliantly colourful upon discovery as they had been 3,000 years earlier, depict a joyful existence that emphasized youth and beauty. Their renderings of flowers, animals, and young men and women are representative of their love of life.

While Minoan art and craftsmanship are acknowledged as some of the most splendid in human history, the people also developed a system of script called Linear A, used primarily in royal and religious communication. They were accomplished engineers and architects as well. Their buildings exhibit intimate knowledge of geometry and physics with enclosed drainage and water conducting systems that set a standard for centuries.

The great palace at Knossos was the centre of Minoan life and culture. Archaeologists discovered an expanse of more than six acres (24,000 square metres) and a structure of 1,300 rooms connected by corridors and

ABOVE: This decorative vase was recovered from an ancient Minoan site. (Creative Commons Olaf Tausch via Wikipedia)

walkways constructed up to three levels high. The complex also included a grand throne room and a courtyard that stretched many yards in length. Workshops, storage rooms, stables, granaries, and offices were located throughout. The palace not only served as the residence of the king and queen, but also as a religious centre where the priests and their attendants lived.

The entire palace was adorned with vivid paintings that covered the walls. Depictions of the Minoan "mother goddess," the central figure of their religion, were visible in several areas, as were images of a fantastic game that shows young people leaping over the heads of bulls. The bull was considered a symbol of the male spirit, and the leaping was apparently a contest that demonstrated the ability of youth and strength to take risk and emerge unscathed.

The palace at Knossos was built across an earthquake fault line along the northeastern coast of Crete, and was destroyed at least twice only to be rebuilt. Knossos during the golden age of the Minoans from roughly 2000 BC to 1400 BC was a bustling centre of commerce and trade with a population of 100,000 or more, a tremendous number of people for the age. Other cities of note included Mallia and Phaistos, where palaces and fine buildings were also constructed.

The decline of Minoan civilization is believed to have occurred around 1400 BC

BOVE: The ruins of the Minoan palace at Knossos continue to inspire. This image is of the north portico.
(Creative Commons Bernard Gagnon via Wikipedia)

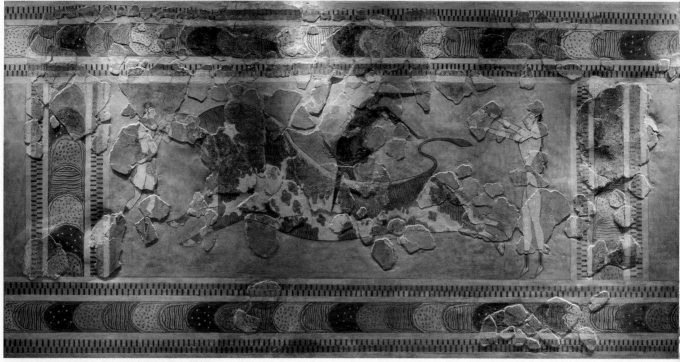

ABOVE: This bright fresco from the palace at Knossos depicts bull leaping. (Creative Commons Jebulon via Wikipedia)

ABOVE: This exquisite Mycenaean death mask is known as the Mask of Agamemnon.
(Creative Commons Xuan Che via Wikipedia)

and to have been precipitated by an immense volcanic eruption on the island of Santorini, where the Minoans had also settled. The destruction was widespread, and since Crete is located only 75 miles south of Santorini there is no doubt that volcanic residue and perhaps a seismically generated tidal wave wrought devastation across all the islands inhabited by the Minoans. Some scholars relate that the destruction gave rise to the tale of the lost continent of Atlantis, thought to have been consumed by an angry sea.

Approximately 500 years before the catastrophe that befell Minoan civilization, the Mycenaeans descended into mainland Greece with gusto. They were known as a warlike race that brought the early Greek language and the worship of Zeus along with them. They dominated the subsistence farming communities of the mainland and built fortified cities at Mycenae, from whence their name is derived, as well as at Argos, Pylos, Tiryns, Thebes, Sparta, Athens, and other locations.

The Mycenaeans, glorified centuries later in the poems of Homer, were the Greeks of the Trojan War. While they were indeed fierce warriors, the Mycenaeans were accomplished artisans in their own right. In the city of Mycenae, German archaeologist Heinrich Schliemann conducted excavations in the late 19th century, uncovering stunning artefacts wrought in gold and other precious materials in the tombs of ancient royalty. As these chalices, death masks, bowls and other objects revealed a high standard of living, they also provided a link to the Minoans. The beauty and precision of the Mycenaean artisans shared elements of craftsmanship known to the Minoans of Crete, and the logical conclusion is that at least some of the work is an amalgam of the two.

As their influence spread, the Mycenaeans may have expanded their rule to Crete itself at least for a time prior to the great volcanic eruption. They built large palaces, although they were not on the scale or as opulent as those of the Minoans, built around a large central hall with adjacent buildings constructed for various purposes. One interesting feature of the Mycenaean

palace was the washroom just off the main entrance, which allowed travellers or those returning from the hunt to freshen up after a ride through the dusty countryside. As recently as the early 1950s, the Mycenaean civilization was the source of great curiosity and discovery. Tablets recovered at multiple sites bore script that was labelled Linear B, which for a time remained unreadable.

With the demise of the Minoans, Mycenaean hegemony spread across the Greek Isles, and favourable trade routes were plied. Colonies were established elsewhere in the Mediterranean, and for a time commerce flourished. However, by 1200 BC encroachment on seaborne trade routes had begun to strangle the source of Mycenaean affluence. And then, on the heels of the civilization's grandeur came an enigmatic era, one of which little is actually known. Therefore, it is recalled as the Dark Age of ancient Greece.

ABOVE: Mycenaean soldiers march toward battle in this scene adorning a vase from 1200 BC.
(Creative Commons Sharon Mollerus via Wikipedia)

ABOVE: This impressive bull was discovered in a grave i the city of Mycenae. (Creative Commons Bkwillwm via Wikipedia)

THE DARK AGE

ABOVE: The ruins of this Dorian site are located on the island of Crete. (Creative Commons Bernard Gagnon via Wikipedia)

The Dark Age of Greek history is so name due to an absence of written documentation from the period, which is generally considered to have stretched 400 years from approximately 1200 BC to 800 BC. Since relatively little is known of the period, research and archaeological exploration are ongoing. As recently as the late 20th century, discoveries relating to its origin and characteristics were revealing additional information and fuelling modern debate.

What is known of the Dark Age involves a collection of fact, myth, theory and conjecture. The collapse of the Bronze Age occurred concurrently with the ebb of Mycenaean civilization, and Greece was not unique in its transition. The great Hittite civilization of the Near East and the New Kingdom of Egypt experienced upheaval as well. Historians have offered several theories for the onset of the Dark Age, including overwhelming internal strife that eroded any cohesion and central government while inciting numerous civil conflicts that destroyed Mycenaea from within to an invasion of the sea peoples or the conquest of the Mycenaeans by the Greek-speaking Dorian tribe.

There is no documented origin for the sea peoples other than a few references from Egyptian sources, and scholars have suggested that these were a confederation of tribes, perhaps from southern Europe, islands of the Aegean Sea, the Black Sea, or Asia Minor, that raided throughout the Mediterranean Basin near the end of the Bronze Age. The notion of the sea peoples was first put forward in the mid-19th century, and the basis for its verity remains an open question.

ABOVE: These richly adorned amphora are representative of the skill of Mycenaean artisans.

(Creative Commons sailko via Wikipedia)

Much of the discourse on the Dark Age centres on the Dorian people, ethnic Greeks, who invaded, or as some historians assert, occupied the mainland of the Attic and Peloponnesian peninsulas from the north or the region of the Balkans sometime around 1100 BC. The Dorians swept away the remnants of the Bronze Age and introduced weapons of iron to mainland Greece. A harder metal that was cheaper to produce, iron became the material of choice in warfare and in the production of tools and farm implements.

Proponents of the Dorian invasion theory suggest that the people were nomadic to an extent due to dependence on their livestock which required new pasture lands regularly. They were described as warlike and merciless, their superior iron weapons overcoming the bronze of the Mycenaeans. These scholars further concluded that the presence of war precipitated the loss of population and the starvation that subsequently set in when farms were abandoned. Those who were displaced then became refugees, traveling from place to place before finally settling in distant locations. The collapse of Mycenaean civilization, they reasoned, was caused by the onslaught of the invaders intent on conquest.

The Dorian invasion, therefore, supposedly led to the abandonment of numerous major population centres, dispersing many peoples to distant locales or into the countryside to live

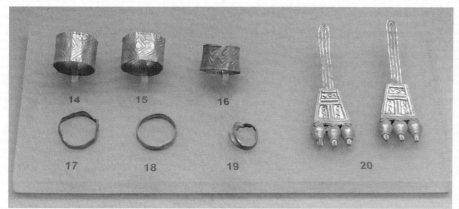

ABOVE: These pieces of jewellery were recovered from the Aeropagus of Athens and date to roughly 850 BC.
(Creative Commons Dorieo via Wikipedia)

ABOVE: This image from the temple of Medinet Habu depicts captive sea people being led by an Egyptian soldier. (Creative Commons Oltau via Wikipedia)

ABOVE: These terra cotta boots were made for the cremation and burial of a woman around 900 BC.
(Creative Commons Sharon Mollerus via Wikipedia)

as subsistence farmers again, and there is some evidence that famine and suffering occurred on a broad scale. It is believed that much of the system of writing in Linear B script was lost, and when writing and literacy re-emerged later the Phoenician alphabet was adopted and customized for Greek use. The rigid class structure of the Mycenaean period fell away during the Dark Age, and later gave rise to the new schools of social and political thought.

During the period of the Dorian invasion, some of the Greek settlements managed to maintain their own identity, and Athens appears to have been one of them. At the same time, Sparta developed from a distinctly Dorian heritage, which undoubtedly contributed to the later rivalry between the two preeminent city states, their difficulty in cooperating with one another, and their eventual armed conflict.

Those cities that were overrun or absorbed by the Dorians experienced an exodus of their populations, and those who fled were either assimilated into the peoples that managed to maintain some degree of independence or emigrated to new lands in a wave of colonization. Many of them ventured to islands in the Aegean or settled in Asia Minor along the coastline of modern day Turkey. In this manner, they exported elements of their Mycenaean culture and kept the oral histories of their ancestors alive.

The catalyst for the Dorian invasion and the onset of the Dark Age may well have been political and social unrest that resulted from economic hardship due to crop failures,

social inequity, or other circumstances. As it was, the lot of the average farmer or villager may have changed little during the period, and while the Dorian invasion was probably a contributing factor to the onset of the Dark Age, some historians assert that it was not necessarily the principal cause of it.

An accompanying story from mythology relates that the Dorian invasion was intertwined with the return to Greece of the sons of Heracles (Roman Hercules), known as the Heracleidae. The story goes that the land of Greece was actually owned by Heracles, and the peoples became allied with one another. The Dorians were said to have been forced out of their homeland and were encouraged by the sons of Heracles to take control of the Peloponnese.

While there is evidence that civilization did survive the hardships of the Dark Age, the loss of literacy has caused the gap in knowledge and theory to remain substantial. Even with the destruction of most of the Mycenaean population centres, there is support for the fact that these areas were later reoccupied. The grand structures were not rebuilt, but some of the remnants remained in use, and aspects of residual Mycenaean are known to have persisted beyond the Dorian invasion, including burial rituals and the features of pottery recovered during archaeological digs.

During the latter 20th century, scholars have begun to re-evaluate the validity of a

true Dorian invasion. Archaeology work that originally was intended to confirm such an event has instead given rise to challenging theories about the coming of the Dark Age. Therefore, those numerous elements of Mycenaean culture that were originally attributed to the waves of invasion that supposedly took place are being reconsidered as possibly organic to the Mycenaeans. If so, it is plausible that the Dorians migrated into mainland Greece in the midst of the erosion of the Mycenaean civilization.

Some observers have even begun to take issue with the term "Dark Age," acknowledging the dearth of a written record but noting that archaeology has revealed a substantial amount of information on the period. Nevertheless, the hallmarks of a collapsing civilization are there in the close examination of Mycenaea. The features of a central administration ceased to exist, while the population declined and elements of the culture either diminished, lost their prominence, or disappeared completely.

By 800 BC, however, there were stirrings of revival in Greece.

ABOVE: The ruins of a Mycenaean wall and gateway provide perspective on a once thriving civilization.
(Creative Commons Joyofmuseums via Wikipedia)

THE ARCHAIC PERIOD

The Archaic Period of Greek history may best be described as a time of rebirth. Emerging from the Dark Age, the Greeks laid the foundation for the Classical Period that followed. From approximately 700 BC to 480 BC, sweeping change, an awakening, occurred among the Greek peoples.

Elements of cohesive societies began to take shape during the Archaic Period, and the city states of Athens, Sparta, Thebes, and Corinth established themselves as preeminent. The city states shared common language and revived writing through the adoption of the Phoenician alphabet, modifying it to recognize vowel sounds which were absent in the original.

The great historian Herodotus wrote of this milestone, "These Phoenicians…brought with them to Hellas (Greece), among many other kinds of learning, the alphabet, which had been unknown before this, I think, to the Greeks. As time went on the sound and the form of the letters were changed. At this time the Greeks… after being taught the letters by the Phoenicians used them with a few changes of form. In so doing, they gave to these characters the name of Phoenician, as was quite fair seeing that the Phoenicians had brought them into Greece."

The city states had become proficient in administration with the collection of taxes, organization of standing armies, and institutions of government. With economies

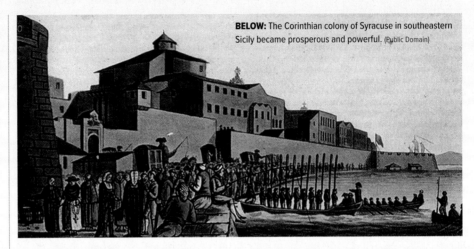

BELOW: The Corinthian colony of Syracuse in southeastern Sicily became prosperous and powerful. (Public Domain)

that were centred on agriculture, land remained a precious commodity. The city states were usually governed by aristocratic councils, or oligarchies, that restricted participation, although the era of kings, characteristic of the Dark Age, had virtually ceased. Still, the poor subsistence farmer was trapped in a form of servitude as the aristocrats kept their hold on power.

Aristotle, the great scientist and philosopher, wrote, "The poor with their wives and children were enslaved to the rich. There was conflict between the nobles and the people for a long time."

Generationally, the balance of power began to shift. With population growth, trade in finished goods and agriculture products began to develop. With such economic evolution new wealth was created and gave rise to a merchant class, its affluence providing a platform to question the authority of the oligarchies. The poor and the newly affluent often banded together to challenge aristocratic authority, and from these stirrings the tyrants, populist leaders who rose in opposition to the establishment, came to power in many city states. The development of the concept of democracy may also be traced to the Archaic Period.

At the same time, the demand for land sparked military conflicts between the city states as well as a surge of migration into areas of Greece that were formerly sparsely inhabited and elsewhere in the Mediterranean world. Greek colonies were founded in Asia Minor, North Africa, mainland Italy, Sicily, and elsewhere, eventually numbering more than 1,500 settlements by 700 BC. Some of the Greeks were seafaring peoples, and they ventured across the sea, first to the Bay of Naples in Italy around 750 BC.

Among the most famous of the early Greek colonies was Syracuse, the second major settlement, founded around 733 BC on the southeastern coast of Sicily.

Syracuse was founded by colonists from Corinth and became a powerful city state in its own right. Economic prosperity and a strong military in alliance with Sparta and Corinth brought prestige, and Syracuse was once among the most powerful Greek cities in the Mediterranean. Interestingly, the colonies maintained ties to their original city states but were not governed by them, developing their own systems of government and becoming independent in dealing with foreign dominions and trading partners. At the height of its power, for example, Syracuse was drawn into protracted conflict with Carthage, a powerful city state of North Africa. At times

ABOVE: Phoenician traders sailed far and wide and brought their alphabet to Greece during the Archaic Period. (Public Domain)

ABOVE: Croesus shows his treasure to Solon in this 17th century painting by Frans Francken the Younger. (Public Domain)

erupting into warfare, the contentiousness persisted for more than 300 years.

Contact with the wider world further included trade and commerce with Egypt and the Eastern regions of Mesopotamia and Lydia in Asia Minor. From the Lydians, the Greeks initiated the widespread use of gold and silver coinage. Concurrent with such expansion, the concept of Greek and particularly Athenian ideals emerged across the known world. Herodotus describes the Athenian perspective in a striking story related to the elusive ideal of happiness.

Once while traveling, Solon, a prominent citizen of Athens, was invited to stay in the lavish palace of Croesus, king of Lydia, at Sardis. Croesus was quite proud of his wealth and royal status, ruling the people of Lydia as an autocrat. He showed Solon a room filled with gold and then asked Solon who he believed was the most fortunate man he had encountered during his lengthy travels. Solon's response was not what Croesus expected.

Herodotus notes that Solon named Tellus, a statesman of Athens, as the happiest man he had ever known. Tellus is a figure representative of the true Athenian and his love for the city state that had nurtured his personal freedom, prosperity for his family, and a sense of community.

"Tellus," wrote Herodotus, "had both beautiful and good children…and he saw all his grandchildren from birth and all remaining alive…And the end of his life was most brilliant: for when the Athenians had a war against their neighbours in Eleusis, coming to the rescue and making a rout of the enemy, he died most beautifully, and the Athenians had buried him publicly right where he fell and honoured him greatly."

Tellus, therefore, exemplified the Greek ideal of the life well lived, an existence that perpetuated a legacy beyond that of financial wealth. Tellus revered the city state and raised his family within it. In the end, he was pleased to give his life to preserve it, placing Athens above his own welfare.

The Archaic Period is further identified with the resurgence of the arts. The poet Homer penned his famous Iliad and Odyssey, epic poems that tell the story of the Trojan War and the voyages of Odysseus (Ulysses), during that time. Greek culture began to flourish and spread across the Aegean and throughout the Mediterranean. Advances in science and mathematics occurred, among them the famous theorem of Pythagoras, which states that the square of the hypotenuse of a right triangle is equal to the sum of the squares of the other two sides. Two thousand years before Isaac Newton, Anaximandros proposed basic principles of gravity and recognized that the earth floated in space and was not fixed or supported atop anything else.

Greek artisans and craftsmen developed new styles of sculpture, pottery, and other forms of art. Sculptors created the Kouroi, the perfectly proportioned form of the youthful male, often nude with hands at his sides and striding forward. The Korai, freestanding female figures, were usually depicted with arms slightly extended and a faint smile, their clothing either heavy or light as preferences changed. These sculptures serve as expressions of the Greek ideal of the human figure and were often seen as honouring the gods or as tributes to the dead.

During the Archaic Period, the Greek peoples experienced a broad renewal of political, economic, philosophical, and technological advances. These great strides served as a springboard for the magnificence of the coming Classical Period.

ABOVE: King Croesus of Lydia was surprised by Solon's answer regarding the happiest man he knew.
(Creative Commons Marco Prins via Wikipedia)

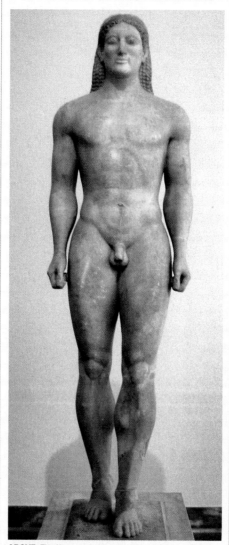

ABOVE: The Kouros became the image of the youthful male as sculpted in the Archaic Period. (Public Domain)

ABOVE: This example of the Korai sculpture of the Archaic Period expresses the Greek ideal of the youthful female. (Creative Commons sailko via Wikipedia)

JASON AND THE ARGONAUTS

Descendant of the messenger god Hermes, Jason is an early figure of Greek mythology. The story of his quest for the golden fleece was probably first told around 1300 BC, and in various versions it has survived through time and exists today most commonly in the version told in the 3rd century BC by Appolonius, the chief librarian at the fabled library of Alexandria.

According to the myth, Jason is the son of Aeson, the legitimate king of Iolcos, an ancient city in Thessaly. Aeson's brother, Pelias, usurped the throne, killing the descendants of Aeson to solidify his grip on power. Alcimede, wife of Aeson, had given birth to Jason, who was in danger. To conceal her son from Pelias, she ordered handmaidens to weep in a tight circle around the baby as though he had been stillborn.

Pelias was warned by an oracle to beware of a man wearing one sandal who might threaten his ill-gotten hold on the throne. Indeed, when Jason was a grown man, having been raised and tutored by the centaur Chiron, a creature half man half horse, he appeared at the court of

ABOVE: King Pelias of Iolcus meets Jason, recognizing him because of his missing sandal. (Public Domain)

ABOVE: Jason returns to King Pelias with the golden fleece in this 4th century BC depiction. (Public Domain)

Pelias wearing one sandal after losing the other while crossing the River Anauros. He informed Pelias that the throne was rightfully his. Pelias replied that in order to take the throne Jason would be required to find and secure the golden fleece, once possessed by the winged ram Chrysomallos and imbued with power and royal authority.

Jason accepts the task, and his quest for the golden fleece is an archetypal adventure. Sailing aboard his ship Argo, Jason and his crew encounter many obstacles, killing the Harpies that plague King Phineus in Thrace, braving the clashing rocks of the Symplegades, slaying the children of the dragon's teeth, overcoming the sleepless dragon that guards the golden fleece, and more. All the while, various gods assist or challenge Jason and the Argonauts. Hera, queen of the Olympian gods and both sister and wife of Zeus, the king of the gods, persuades Aphrodite and her son Eros to make Medea, daughter of King Aeetes of Colchis and granddaughter of the sun god Helios, fall in love with Jason.

Medea, in turn, assists Jason in taking the golden fleece from Aeetes amid murder and

mayhem as Aeetes pursues them in vain. During the return voyage to Iolcos, the Argo is beset by storms, the Argonauts must pass the tempting Sirens whose song entices unlucky sailors to crash their ships on rocky shores, and Medea subdues the giant bronze man Talos at Crete.

When the adventurers reach Iolcos, Medea tricks the daughters of Pelias into murdering their father, and she is exiled with Jason to Corinth, where their relationship disintegrates. Jason becomes engaged to Creusa, daughter Corinthian King Creon. Filled with rage, Medea kills Creusa with a dress that bursts into flames as she wears it, and Creon is burned to death as he attempts to save her. For good measure, Medea murders the two sons that Jason has fathered with her. She escapes Jason's wrath in a chariot sent by Helios.

Jason later reclaims the throne of Iolcus but has lost favour with Hera because his promise to always love Medea is broken. He dies alone while sleeping under the stern of the old decaying Argo, which caves in upon him.

The fractured union of Jason and Medea is the basis for the ancient play Medea written by the famous tragedian Euripides.

ABOVE: Jason and Medea are shown in this 1907 painting by artist John William Waterhouse. (Public Domain)

THE TROJAN WAR

The Trojan War serves as the foundation for much of the perspective of Western history. Herodotus, the father of history, tells the story of the conflict between the Mycenaean Greeks and the Trojans, who occupy a great city on the coast of Asia Minor. Four hundred years after the decade-long war, the poet Homer wrote the Iliad and the Odyssey, classics of Western literature, recounting may vignettes of the war itself and of the adventures of Odysseus on his return voyage to the island of Ithaca.

Into modern times, scholars have debated whether the Trojan War actually occurred. However, it is relevant to understand that for the ancient Greek audience that Herodotus, Homer and others addressed the war was indeed real. Their stories of the struggles of men and gods, of intrigue and betrayal, of heroism and cowardice were integral components of their religious practices. Even so, sceptical observers such as Thucydides doubted that the war was conducted on such a grand scale as reported. While he questioned whether nearly 1,200 ships filled to the brim with Greek warriors would have crossed the Aegean Sea, Thucydides stopped short of denying that a war did take place. Further, the tragedian playwright Euripides is well known for embellishment and changing the facts of a situation to fit his poetic narrative.

Nevertheless, after years of dismissal by modern historians and scientists, a shift was noted during the 19th century. Beyond the idea of the Trojan War, scientific debate had persisted as to whether Troy itself actually existed. Archaeological excavations, however, did reveal enough evidence to conclude that Troy, a great city of ancient Anatolia, did actually exist. In fact, several cities were constructed on top of one another, and scientists point to either Troy VI or Troy VII as the likely candidate for the city that was involved in the war with the Mycenaean Greeks.

Covering an expanse of roughly 270,000 square metres encircled by a defensive ditch cut into surrounding rock, Troy VI appears to date to around 1250 BC, the approximate time of the Trojan War, probably just prior to the collapse of Mycenaea. There is evidence that the city was destroyed, including residue of burned wood, arrowheads and spear points of bronze and even weapons embedded into the walls that suggests some level of armed conflict had occurred.

Chief among those who searched for historical Troy was German archaeologist and businessman Heinrich Schliemann. Although he was an amateur archaeologist, Schliemann pursued his avocation with vigour, actually seeking the location of historical Troy. Following the work of English archaeologist Frank Calvert, who identified the site of the ancient Turkish city of Hissarlik as the location of Troy, Schliemann began his own excavations in 1870, although he was unconvinced that Hissarlik corresponded to the city described by Herodotus and Homer.

Schliemann found some shards of pottery, tools of copper and bronze, moulds for implements, and then on the day before he intended to cease his excavations, gold. According to contemporary sources, Schliemann believed he had come across the treasure of Trojan King Priam, and during the next few years no fewer than nine

ABOVE: German archaeologist Heinrich Schliemann advocated that the works of Homer related to historic events. In the early 1870s he did much of the early excavation of the Turkish site of what is now generally accepted to have been Troy.

ABOVE: Heinrich Schliemann discovered the magnificent Mask of Agamemnon during 1876 excavations at Mycenae. (Creative Commons DieBuche via Wikipedia)

separate cities were discovered. Although Schliemann's work has been criticized for its disregard for preservation and thorough archaeological procedures that corrupted the site to an extent, his discovery engendered a wave of re-examination.

Schliemann referred to his most compelling evidential layer as the "burnt city," but it appears to date to at least 1,000 years earlier than the Troy of the great war. Nevertheless, the logical conclusion was that Troy did in fact exist and that one of the cities discovered by Schliemann was actually the city of lore and legend – long buried with its clues to the past. Schliemann went on to excavate cities of Mycenaean Greece and in 1876 discovered the famed golden mask of Agamemnon at Mycenae. Agamemnon was identified by Homer as the

ABOVE: The walls of late Bronze Age Troy are visible today in modern Turkey. (Creative Commons CherryX via Wikipedia)

ABOVE: These ancient figures of musicians are located in the Museum of Troy. (Creative Commons Dosseman via Wikipedia)

peoples. The existence of a great city across the Aegean may have given rise to a raid intended to seize the city and plunder its riches.

In either case, though, there is little support as of yet for the mounting of a military expedition of such immense proportion as described by the ancients, and the notion of a 10-year siege defies logic. Most cities like Troy probably could not withstand such a prolonged siege without exhausting food, water and other supplies.

Regardless, the story of the Trojan War supplied the Greeks of later periods with an explanation of their place in history. The epic poetry of Homer and the histories of Herodotus gave the people a sense of themselves, which is a vital element of civilization. Interestingly, the poet Vergil did the same for the Romans with the Aeneid, which recounts the journey of the Trojan warrior Aeneas, who escapes from the burning Troy and eventually makes landfall in Italy, becoming the ancestor of Romulus and Remus, the founders of Rome, and the first great hero of that civilization.

King of Mycenae who led the confederation of Greek states against Troy, sailing across the Aegean and laying siege to the city for 10 years. Many of the treasures Schliemann discovered through the years are now on display at the British Museum in London.

As for the verdict on Troy's existence, scientific study and excavation that began in the late 20th century have revealed that certain geological evidence and the descriptions of geographical features, such as the contours of coastlines and the presence of high ground and low-lying areas essentially match the descriptions of Troy's location found in the ancient histories.

Additional research centred on the Egyptian and Hittite civilizations of the Mediterranean and the Near East add to the effort to establish Troy as real or mythical and to whether the Trojan War actually did occur near the end of the Bronze Age. Inscriptions carved by the ancient Hittites make reference to a conflict involving a city they refer to as "Wilusa," which is believed to be Troy, as well as a kingdom called "Ahhiyawa," which is almost certainly Mycenaean Greece. While inconclusive in themselves, these inscriptions contribute to the mounting circumstantial evidence that points to Troy's existence. Other explanations indicate the possibility of some type of armed conflict, perhaps civil war, that generated among the Hittites themselves, which included the Trojans as participants. Nevertheless, such recent contributions stir the desire of scientists and archaeologists to approach a new era of discovery and analysis.

While the ancient Greek historians provide fantastic explanations for the cause of the Trojan War, there are other credible theories on the topic. Troy, for example, was one of several powerful cities that might exert control of the Dardanelles and the Bosporus, the straits of passage from the Black Sea to the Aegean. Control of these waterways would allow Troy to dominate prominent trade routes to and

from the East. Therefore, the idea of a war spurred by trade – a key element of Mycenaean economic prosperity – is plausible. Additionally, the Mycenaean Greeks are known to have been militaristic

ABOVE: The ruins of the east gate and houses of Troy VI are visible in this image. (Creative Commons Bgabel via Wikipedia)

ABOVE: In this 16th century painting by Federico Barocci, the Trojan warrior Aeneas flees burning Troy. (Public Domain)

HOMER

The epic poems of the Iliad and the Odyssey, telling the stories of the decade-long siege of Troy and the ultimate victory of the Mycenaean Greeks in the Trojan War as well as the long and perilous journey of the king of Ithaca, Odysseus, from the war in Anatolia back to his home among the Greek Isles, are attributed through the millennia to the blind poet Homer. However, speculation persists as to author's life and even his actual existence.

It is believed that the two great works of Western literature were completed sometime in the 7th or 8th century BC, but little is actually known of the historic Homer. Some academics even assert that the name of Homer or the descriptive adjective "Homeric" actually relate to a specific period of Greek literature rather than an individual. Others disagree. They hold true to the belief that Homer was an individual who indeed lived and wrote the epic adventures of the Iliad and the Odyssey. Another school of thought relates that the two works were authored by multiple poets rather than a single individual, adding that the narrative was edited and refined, maturing through the years.

While it is universally acknowledged that the Iliad and the Odyssey have shaped the culture of ancient Greece and in turn Western civilization as a whole, speculation on the life of Homer provides an interesting adjunct to their study and appreciation. Numerous accounts of Homer's life were told and retold in ancient times, but the most commonly known relates that he was born in Ionia, a region of Anatolia with Greek ancestry and located in modern-day Turkey. He was said to have been blind, losing his sight sometime during his adulthood, and he is thought to have lived on the Greek island of Chios in the northern Aegean Sea. By the 5th century BC, Smyrna, another Anatolian coastal city, was also contending that the great poet was a resident.

Accounts of Homer's parentage differ. The Roman tradition states that he was the grandson of Odysseus and of Nestor, a legendary king of Pylos. His father, then, was Telemachus, the son of Odysseus and his mother Epicaste, the daughter of Nestor. Another relates that Homer was the son of the nymph Critheis and that his father was named as the River Meles to perhaps conceal a scandalous report that he was conceived out of wedlock. His death is equally shrouded in mystery, and one story goes that he died after failing to solve a riddle.

Several biographies of Homer emerged in ancient times, including Life of Homer, written by an unknown author who is referred to as Pseudo-Herodotus. Although the biographical text states that it was written by Herodotus, it is not considered to have actually been one of his works. Another description is contained in the Contest of Homer and Hesiod, a work probably written in the 2nd century AD based on earlier scroll texts that predate it by approximately 300 to 400 years.

Other works were attributed to Homer during ancient times, but today only the

ABOVE: The life of the Greek poet Homer is one of mystery to modern scholars. (Public Domain)

Iliad and the Odyssey are directly linked to his shadowy existence. To date, there is no record at the local level to indicate that a poet of Homer's supposed fame and status actually lived in the areas he might have been thought to inhabit. Nevertheless, by the 3rd and 2nd centuries BC ancient Greeks strove to affirm his existence through the available biographical works that were – quite probably – replete with fiction.

ABOVE: Homer wears a laurel crown in this painting by Raphael from the 16th century. (Public Domain)

LEFT: This 1874 painting by William-Adolphe Bouguereau is titled Home and his Guide. (Public Domain)

THE ILIAD AND THE ODYSSEY

History credits the blind poet Homer with authorship of the Iliad and the Odyssey, the stirring accounts of the Trojan War and the adventures of Ithican King Odysseus during his return from the legendary conflict. The two epic poems remain pillars of classic literature and blend fact, fiction, and fantasy into timeless tales.

Written in approximately 750 BC and 725 BC, the Iliad and the Odyssey served as significant influences on Greek thought, noble ideals, pride, and interaction with the pantheon of gods that they worshipped. Each describes archetypal heroes and describes their exploits while also laying bare their base attributes. The gods play key roles in the outcome of the war, and their interference in the affairs of mankind is seen throughout the works.

The Iliad covers a period of only 52 days of the final year during the decade-long Trojan War, describing the tumultuous events that bring about its conclusion. The cause of the war is apparently common knowledge to the readers of the Iliad. According to Greek

mythology, Paris, prince of Troy, has abducted Helen, the most beautiful woman in the world, following his judgment of the fairest of the goddesses among Hera, Athena, and Aphrodite. Paris chose Aphrodite, awarding her a golden apple, and proceeded to claim his own prize promised by the goddess of love – Helen, who was already married to Menelaus, king of Sparta. Paris abducts Helen and carries her off to Troy, sparking the Trojan War as Menelaus persuades his brother, King Agamemnon of Mycenae, to raise a confederation of Greek armed forces to retrieve Helen and punish the Trojans.

The Trojan War supposedly ends with the Greeks feigning withdrawal after years of inconclusive struggle, leaving a great wooden horse before the gates of Troy apparently as a gift acknowledging the Trojans as worthy adversaries. However, Odysseus has devised a plan to hide warriors inside the horse, and when the Trojans drag it within their impregnable walled city, the Greeks wait until nightfall before exiting the horse and wreaking havoc, destroying Troy as the fleet

ABOVE: Trojan Prince Paris and Helen are seen in this painting. The abduction of Helen sparked the Trojan War according to Greek mythology. (Public Domain)

has turned back to Trojan shores and the gates of the city are opened to them. Troy is burned to the ground.

Homer seems to realize that his audience is already familiar with the beginning of the Trojan War and its end with the ruse of the Trojan Horse. He devotes his opening to a hymn to the muse. He writes, "Sing, O muse, of the rage of Achilles, son of Peleus, that brought countless ills upon the Achaeans (Greeks)." Achilles is the greatest warrior of the Greeks, but Agamemnon angered him by confiscating a concubine from him. Therefore, Achilles initially refuses to fight the Trojans.

All the while, the gods are watching. Hera and Athena demand the destruction of Troy, and Zeus, king of the gods, has already assented with the caveat that he will one day destroy Greek cities as he sees fit, including Mycenae, home of Agamemnon. Aphrodite has intervened to save Paris, who takes on Menelaus in one-on-one combat and nearly loses his life. As Menelaus drags Paris by the head to his apparent doom, Aphrodite loosens the straps of Paris's helmet and takes him up into a cloud to make good his escape.

Vignettes of the Iliad include the terrible losses suffered by the Greeks in the absence of Achilles, his subsequent entry into the fight, and the loss of his childhood friend Patroclus at the hands of Hector, the Trojan hero and son of King Priam, who is assisted by the god Apollo. Achilles slays Hector in retribution for the death of his friend, and the fate of Troy is sealed. Achilles ties the corpse of Hector to his chariot, dragging the body around the city walls, and forcing Priam to beg for his son's remains.

ABOVE: Achilles slays Hector in this 17th century painting by artist Peter Paul Rubens. (Public Domain)

ABOVE: This 19th century painting depicts the wrath of Achilles during the Trojan War. (Public Domain)

Homer ends the Iliad here, allowing the rest of the story, including the death of Achilles and the story of the Trojan horse, to be told and retold by others.

The Odyssey takes up the long journey of Odysseus and his soldiers back to Ithaca. In defeating the Trojans, the Greeks did incur the wrath of numerous powerful gods and goddesses. Therefore, their homeward trek is fraught with danger. The fleet is battered by a storm, and then Homer describes the tribulations of the hero's wife and son, Queen Penelope and Prince Telemachus, as suitors besiege the Ithacan palace, convinced that Odysseus is dead and intent on taking Penelope as their bride.

During his fantastic voyage, Odysseus is held prisoner by the nymph Calypso on a remote island until Zeus orders he to set him free. Among other adventures, the Ithacan hero and his crew face the dreaded cyclopes Polyphemus, blinding him and escaping from imprisonment in his cave as the giant hurls boulders at their

ship. Landing at Aeaea, the seafarers come under the spell of the goddess Circe, a sorceress and daughter of Helios, the sun god. Circe welcomes the visitors but offers a potion that turns the Ithacan crewmen into swine. However, Hermes, messenger of the gods, has provided Odysseus with the herb moly, making him immune, and he successfully compels her to return his men to their human form.

Odysseus visits Hades for further directions to his home, and then returns to Circe, who warns him to beware of the Sirens, whose enchanting song lures seamen to their deaths on the rocky shore of their island. He instructs the men to lash him to his ship's mast and to plug their ears with wax. They pass safely and then negotiate past the six-headed monster Scylla and the deadly whirlpool Charybdis.

Other adventures and trials befall the voyagers before Odysseus safely returns to

Ithaca, at first disguised but then revealing himself to his loyal son, Telemachus, as the two tearfully embrace. Odysseus instructs Telemachus to remove all weapons from the great hall where the evil suitors are to gather and disguises himself once again. Biding his time before wreaking vengeance on the would-be usurpers, Odysseus reveals himself, slays the suitors to a man, and later executes those disloyal members of his household who had supported them. The halls of the palace are strewn with bodies and rivulets of blood.

Odysseus and Penelope are united once again, and the king defeats the families of the vanquished suitors in a brief war. With the protection and providence of the friendly gods, peace returns to the kingdom of Ithaca and the Odyssey comes to a close.

Throughout his years of tribulation, Odysseus displays the qualities of the archetypal hero, bravery, cunning, perseverance, and poise. Homer extols these virtues, and the Greek people looked to the story as inspiration for their own conduct.

Along with the Iliad, the Odyssey is one of the oldest texts of antiquity to remain the subject of study and in popular circulation, widely read and reviewed in modern days. The epic poems established a standard in Western culture and literature that has become timeless.

ABOVE: In this 19th century painting, Odysseus is overcome with emotion during his epic travels. (Public Domain)

ABOVE: The Greek hero Odysseus is depicted in this mosaic. The story of his return from Troy to Ithaca is told in the Odyssey. (Creative Commons Valdavia via Wikipedia)

ABOVE: Odysseus comes to Penelope prior to dealing with the suitors besieging the palace of Ithaca. (Public Domain)

THE FIRST OLYMPIC GAMES

The sanctuary of Olympia, located in the northeast of the Peloponnesian peninsula, was one of the most sacred religious sites of ancient Greece. It was the centre of the worship of Zeus, king of the gods, and home to dozens of magnificent temples and shrines, including the principal temples of Zeus and Hera, queen of the gods, the complex of Hermes, messenger of the gods, and the Pelipion, tomb of the mythological figure Pelops, namesake of the Peloponnese.

For 12 centuries, Olympia was also the site of the ancient Olympic games, held within the sacred enclosure, or temenos, at the revered shrine. The first Olympics were held in 776 BC, and the popular athletic contests were convened every four years until well into the period of Roman occupation. One of the most important cultural events of ancient Greece, the Olympics emerged from the tradition of funerary games held to honour the dead. Homer writes of such a festival in the Iliad. Those games were called by the great warrior Achilles after the death of Patroclus, his childhood friend, in battle against the Trojans.

Greek mythology credits Zeus with originating the games, while some accounts state that Pelops was the advocate of the festival of physical fitness, an ideal that was an integral component of Greek culture. According to some scholars, the mythological origin of the games came when Zeus wrestled his father, Cronus, for possession of the great throne of the gods. At the same time, Apollo defeated Ares in the boxing arena and ran faster than the

ABOVE: In this painting by Edouard Joseph Dantan an athlete prepares to throw the discus in the ancient Olympic games. (Public Domain)

wing-footed Hermes. Heracles won both the wrestling and other strength competitions.

The Olympics were regularly held during the summer, usually on the first full moon after the summer solstice, placing them sometime in July. They were opened with a great processional from the city of Elis to the sanctuary of Olympia. Every athlete was required to swear an oath to abide by the rules and structure of the games and to compete with honour. They were required to affirm that they had been in training for at least 10 months, and individuals who were known to have committed crimes in the past were excluded.

Organized by the leaders of the city state of Elis, where Olympia is located, the games were intended as a religious and athletic festival. During the games, squabbles between the city states, rivalries and disputes, even armed conflicts, were suspended in the name of athletic competition. The games became so popular that in 480 BC when the Persians invaded Greece the leaders of the city states agreed to raise an allied army to defend their homeland, but only after the Olympic games were concluded. The reason for the delay was logical. It would be difficult to field an army while many of the able-bodied men were immersed in the games.

The Olympic panhellenic truce typically lasted as long as three months, and in time as many as 40,000 spectators and participants crowded into Olympia with the games themselves taking place over a five-day period. The games grew to include wrestling, boxing, chariot racing, distance running, throwing the javelin and discus, and short distance foot races. Eventually, the number of events held over the five days rose to 18.

Olympic champions received crowns of leaves cut from the sacred olive tree of

Zeus, and the finish lines were marked with wreaths also cut from the sacred tree. The winners were sometimes given other awards, such as decorative vases or olive oil contained in amphora, as well.

A single event was held during the first 12 Olympics, and in the first games Koroibos of Elis won the stadion foot race, which was run across one length of the stadium track, approximately 192 metres (600 feet). Athletes were grouped by lot and ran in preliminaries with the winner advancing to the final heat. The name of every champion was recorded during later games, and the record provides one of the first accurate chronologies of ancient Greece. The athletes competed naked, and women were generally prohibited from attending. The games were open to all Greek males, and though the names of the champions were listed, there is no mention of recorded times or distances. Therefore, the emphasis was placed simply on being the best rather than establishing some sort of record or standard for posterity.

One of the events was called pankration, essentially an ancient form of mixed martial arts that combined wrestling and boxing. As with the wrestling competition, the participants were covered with oil.

ABOVE: Athletes take part in an Olympic foot race. in the beginning the race was the only Olympic event. (Public Domain)

ABOVE: Long distance runners compete in the Olympic Games. (Creative Commons RickyBennison via Wikipedia)

ABOVE: A runner finishes his race, exhausted, during the ancient Olympic games. (Public Domain)

ABOVE: This artist's rendering depicts the venue of the Olympic games in the sanctuary of Olympia. (Public Domain)

Competitors in the "combat" sports were instructed to indicate their submission by raising their index fingers, but the competition was so intense at times that one of the fighters died before they were able to quit. The only rules enforced during the pankration competition prohibited biting and gouging. Corporal punishment was meted out to those who committed violations in competition, such as a false start during a foot race. There were no weight or size limitations imposed for physical competitions.

During the first 49 Olympic games, only one judge presided over the competition, deciding outcomes in close races and other administrative tasks. In time, other judges from Elis were trained, and their number increased to 12. Known as the Hellanodikai, the judges were highly respected, distinguishable by the purple robes that they wore, and given seats within the stadium that indicated their honoured position. Judges inherited their posts through family lines at first, but later the positions were filled by drawing lots. Decisions were final and could not be reversed, but the judges themselves were subject to review by a council of elders. If their performance was less than satisfactory, a judge was subject to a fine.

For the first 250 years, the Olympic games were held within the sanctuary area, but through the centuries larger stadiums were built to accommodate the growing crowds. Subsidiary games were held in other locations across Greece, including Nemea, Isthmia, and Delphi, but never achieved the status or popularity of those held at Olympia.

Amid the athletic contests, the religious aspect of the celebration was reverently observed. Sacrifices were performed on the altars of Zeus or of other deities, sometimes involving many head of cattle. Once the sacrifices were completed and the gods had received their portion, the remaining meat was distributed to the people for cooking as part of the great feasts that occurred. When the athletic competition had concluded, 100 cattle were sacrificed at the altar of Zeus in an event called the hetacomb. More than 70 altars are known to have existed in ancient Olympia.

One of the most awe inspiring spectacles that drew crowds during the ancient Olympic games was not on the field of athletic competition. Located in the great temple of Zeus was a tremendous statue of the king of the gods, carved in ivory and adorned with gold by the famed sculptor Phideas in approximately 435 BC. The statue is remembered as one of the seven wonders of the ancient world.

In 385 AD, Roman emperor Theodosius I banned the Olympics, considering them a pagan festival, but the historical record indicates that the games continued in some venues. The modern era of the Olympics began appropriately in Athens in 1896.

ABOVE: This photo depicts archaeological excavations conducted at Olympia during the late 19th century. (Public Domain)

THE CITY STATES

By the end of the Bronze Age, Mycenaean Greece, the Greece of the Trojan War, had passed away for reasons that remain unclear even today. The Dark Age followed, leaving no written record of its history.

While Athens and Sparta, as well as other kingdoms or principalities, had flourished prior to the Dark Age, there remains the void of 300 years. Among scholars, however, there is a belief that at some time during the 8th century BC a north to south migration of Greek peoples occurred. During that time, former settlements were reclaimed, farming was re-established, and in time the population growth that occurred brought about some stabilization of the economic and cultural lives of the inhabitants of the Attic and Peloponnesian peninsulas.

The city state, or polis, then became the cornerstone of the Classical Greece that is remembered and revered so thoroughly in

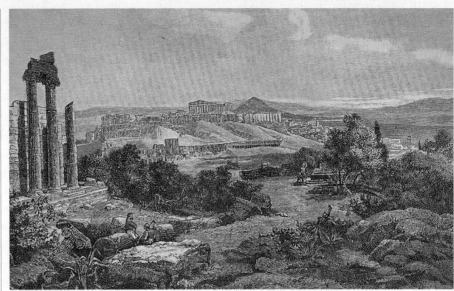

ABOVE: This 19th century engraving of the Attic Plains reveals the fields, hills and mountains of the Greek country that gave rise to the city states. (Public Domain)

ABOVE: This 19th century painting by Leo von Klenze depicts the city of Athens with the Acropolis looming above. (Public Domain)

ABOVE: This reconstruction of the west pediment of the Parthenon shows the contest between Athena and Poseidon. (Creative Commons Tilemahos Efthimiadis via Wikipedia)

the modern era. Trade and commerce were vigorous, and though there was no native written language since the Mycenaean had been lost, the Greeks appropriated the Phoenician alphabet as their own, modified it for their varied dialects, and then came the rudimentary beginnings of a written record.

The concept of the ancient city state was not unique to Greek civilization. Archaeological evidence suggests that such population centres had existed in Phoenicia and Babylonia even earlier. The formation of the Greek city states, though, may be attributed to several factors, including the end of some unknown but lengthy upheaval, the distinctive geography of the region, and that fact that a common ancestry alone may well have been insufficient to prompt the desire to congregate in any larger confederation.

Historians are generally convinced that the most significant factor in the formation

of the city states was the land itself. The geography of Greece is well known for its rugged mountainous interior, peaks rising to staggering heights punctuated by jagged cliffs, long valleys and narrow ravines descending to coastal plains that provided in some locales easy access to the expansive Mediterranean and the adjacent Aegean and Ionian seas as well. Countless clusters of islands push up from the ocean floor as if some giant hand had emptied a bag of jewels into a pool, and many of these were embryonic settlement sites that grew into major city states as well.

Logically, these mountains, valleys, and other geographical features were substantial barriers to the formation of significant population centres. Separate communities took shape in large part because travel between settlements was difficult at best. Even though they shared common aspects of civilization, including

similar language and ancestry, the early Greek city state communities were chiefly isolated from one another. During these early years, agricultural settlements thrived with fertile soil as farmers cultivated the flat plains and the slopes of hillsides. Such isolation was further fostered with increasing economic prosperity. Progressing from subsistence farming, entrepreneurs traded their surplus grain and other crops for finished goods, while the settlements along the coastline may well have gravitated toward the sea with fishing and merchant shipping stimulating trade and exploration.

The Greek city states emerged and then prospered during the Archaic Period of 800 BC to approximately 480 BC, and amid this maturation process, they grew distinctly separate. Larger city states fielded their own armies and perhaps navies. They formed their own governments, built fortifications for defensive purposes, and became independent in their own right. Nevertheless, the common thread of Greek descent and ancestral ties remained in the midst of individual legal, social, cultural, and political dynamics.

At the peak of the growth of the city states, there were more than 1,000 of these settlements, or "poleis," located in Greece proper, across the Mediterranean basin, and in Asia Minor along the coast of modern Turkey. A tremendous wave of colonization had been nurtured by economic prosperity and population growth, and the expansion persisted across approximately 250 years as Greek culture was exported and took root throughout the known Western world. Among the best known city states were Athens, Sparta, Corinth, Elis, Eritrea, Thebes, Rhodes, and Syracuse. Athens grew to more than 200,000 inhabitants by the end of the 5th century BC and was the largest in terms of population, while the smaller city states, such as Corinth and Argos, were probably home to 10,000 to 15,000 people at their peak. Although the peak population of Sparta is estimated at perhaps even fewer, the Spartan city state was the largest in terms of land holdings at roughly 8,500 kilometres (3,300 miles).

As population centres grew, they often exhibited similar physical characteristics. The construction of a fortified citadel was usually completed on high ground in or near the centre of the city. Known as the acropolis, this high ground was usually the site of temples or shrines to various deities,

ABOVE: Ancient Athenian ruins lie below the Temple of Zeus in Athens. (Creative Commons George E. Koronaios via Wikipedia)

ABOVE: This stylish drinking cup dates to the city state of Athens in the 6th century BC. (Creative Commons Wmpearl via Wikipedia)

ABOVE: This 17th century painting depicts the suffering during a plague in the city of Athens. (Public Domain)

ABOVE: The ruins of temples soar above the walls on the Acropolis in Athens. (Creative Commons Chabe01 via Wikipedia)

even though some of the population centres were barely the size of a large village, an early monarch of sorts exerted whatever formal authority might exist.

By the mid-6th century, however, that began to change. The power of the relative few members of the elite was challenged as prosperity began to more clearly define the social classes. The emergence of a merchant class, consisting of those who had amassed some measure of wealth through business endeavours, brought about sharper social distinctions over time and gave rise to a robust discourse regarding class struggle and pre-eminence, particularly in the larger city states. In due course, men of influence, at first from the aristocracy but then increasingly from the emergent merchant class or even the fringes of society came forward and acceded to power. The political strongmen were usually vigorously supported by the population at large. Known as "tyrants," such a description did not originally carry with it the negative connotation that it bears in modern times. The tyrants were quite often moderate and judicious, bringing about stability and order.

The city state of Athens was governed by a monarch called the "basileus" as early as the 9th century BC, and this ruler was believed to avail himself of the counsel of influential nobles. Ironically, though, the monarchy was extinguished in the year 683 BC by those very nobles who had clustered around the basileus in trust. By that time the nobility of Athens had become quite prosperous, reaping tremendous wealth from the export of grain and agricultural products, wine, and olive oil.

The olive tree itself, now a symbol of the prosperity and grandeur of ancient Greece, was to become such a pillar of the Greek city states' economies that it was considered a gift from the gods, quite probably from Athena, the goddess of wisdom, from who Athens had actually taken its name. The olive tree was

some of them built to honour patron gods that the particular city state had adopted. Always, the acropolis was constructed in some prominent location, whether that was outside the heart of the city or actually the central hub of traffic and interaction. The agora, a public marketplace, became common in the late 8th century BC, serving not only as an area where buying and selling took place, but also as a gathering area where issues of the day were discussed and news was often exchanged.

Since political and social involvement were more often occurring within the city state, its influence spread across the surrounding countryside, commonly referred to as the "chora," and the city state became the nexus of government and civil administration, as well as commerce and residence. By the 5th century BC, city states were developing their own legal systems, forming separate distinct governments, issuing coinage, and

even collecting taxes from the citizenry. The phenomenon of colonization produced offspring of the original city states. Time, distance, and a modicum of independent thought spurred these colonial sites to maintain some strong ties with the parent, that is religious or mutually beneficial trade relations, while developing their own autonomous governmental apparatus and political identity.

Aristocratic land owners were the original power brokers of the city states. Early in the development of local governments, they were the authorities – self-appointed often enough – or the "kingmakers" because of their personal wealth and following influence. While the aristocratic class is known to have been opposed to any long-term monarchy, the use of the terms king or queen is somewhat misleading. The political independence of a given city state was something to be cherished and guarded at the same time, and

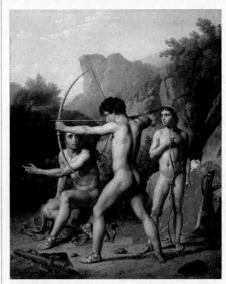

ABOVE: Three Spartan boys practice their archery skills in the militaristic city state. (Public Domain)

ABOVE: This 19th century painting by Giuseppe Diotti is titled 'The Selection of the Infant Spartans.' (Public Domain)

ABOVE: This helmet once belonging to a Spartan soldier now resides in the British Museum.

(Creative Commons John Antoni via Wikipedia)

ABOVE: Lycurgus is remembered as the principal architect of Spartan society. (Public Domain)

a contributor to the Greek quality of life in many ways. While its oil was used as fuel for lamps and believed to have some medicinal value, the fruit itself was a staple of the Greek diet. Its leaves were made into wreaths that crowned the heads of heroes and athletic event champions, and its wood was a necessity in the construction of homes and ships.

Greek mythology offered that the source of the olive tree was indeed divine. It came as the result of a contest proposed by Zeus between Athena and Poseidon, god of the sea. The object was to produce a gift to the people of Athens, and the recipients would choose the one they preferred. Poseidon struck his trident on a sharp outcropping of rock, and a salt spring sprang forth. Athena produced an olive tree filled with ripening fruit, its branches swaying in the gentle breeze. The Athenians chose the olive tree, source of their future economic prosperity, and even today an olive tree is firmly rooted on the Athenian Acropolis in homage to the great gift.

And so, directly from the fruits of their labour, the Athenian nobles also gained significant political influence. They began to meet regularly and dubbed their gatherings the "Aeropagus" in reference to the prominent hill on which they convened. The Aeropagus came to one conclusion that changed the course of history. Rather than vesting all the power and responsibility for the city state in one man, they suggested the formation of a government of nine men elected by their own body. From their initiative, an oligarchy emerged in Athens, and the chosen nine were called "archons." These men were authorized to discuss issues that ran the gamut of Athenian affairs, but their authority to implement change was governed by a caveat that required the approval of the entire Aeropagus. As the oligarchy and the Aeropagus grew in stature, class distinctions remained in Athenian society, and the distribution of wealth was limited. Rumblings from the common farmer were heard as time passed and their once fertile soil was depleted by decades of planting and harvesting. When they were unable to produce crops and feed their families, these poorer inhabitants of Athens were compelled to sell family members or even themselves into indentured servitude. But even as the lower class suffered, the aristocrats continued to prosper.

Then, as growing resentment boiled over into civil disturbance by the mid-7th century BC, the oligarchy lost its grip on the people. In its wake came a succession of the so-called

ABOVE: Lycurgus addresses a meeting of Spartan leaders in the militaristic city state. (Public Domain)

ABOVE: A young woman of Thebes tends her father who has been wounded in battle. (Public Domain)

tyrants, supported in their bid for power by the will of the people.

Among the most influential of the tyrants, Solon rose to prominence in Athens in 594 BC and established an aristocratic government that was formulated around an early constitutional document. Solon was responsive to the concerns of the people and enacted far reaching reforms. He is remembered even in modern times as a champion of the lower classes and as a lawgiver. Through the succession of the oligarchy to the tyrants, the earliest notions of Athenian democracy began to develop.

Sparta, however, swiftly became an influential exception to the concept of rule by the tyrants. According to contemporary historians of ancient Greece, the city state came into being as the military commander and statesman Lycurgus was instructed by the Oracle of Apollo, god of the sun, at Delphi to build a social structure for the city state that was grounded in three basic virtues. These included equality among the citizens of Sparta, military strength, and austerity.

The revered lawgiver of Sparta, Lycurgus presented a constitution, often called the Great Rhetra, to the Spartan people, and it was adopted in approximately 650 BC. The Great Rhetra accomplished several notable tasks, firmly initiating the militaristic social structure that would enable Sparta to become a great power whose warrior way of life remains familiar to this day, preserving the influence and governing power of the aristocracy, and supporting the two royal houses that existed in the city state. Lycurgus was the architect of the Spartan emphasis on the military and service to the city state, requiring self-sacrifice if necessary.

Loyalty to the state was a given, and military service was compulsory. Every Spartan male citizen was required to serve in the army, and they were essentially subject to call-up throughout their lives. Young boys were removed from their homes at the age of just seven and enrolled in the Agoge, an educational system conceived and run by the city state that included physical and military indoctrination and training. All men aged 30 or younger were required to live in military barracks, away from wives and children if they were married, and they were expected to take meals at communal tables. Such a strict regimen built a cohesive fighting force that was at any given time the finest in the world.

Spartan women were well educated and lived in greater freedom than most other city states. Such was probably a necessity to maintain the social fabric in the prolonged absences of the Spartan men. The women went to school and were allowed to independently own property.

While Athens and Sparta came of age, other city states grew in prominence as well. Rhodes was a maritime city state that occupied an island in the eastern Mediterranean. Situated along the busy east-west trade routes, it was home to a merchant class that achieved significant wealth. Thebes became an influential city state and an early rival of Athens. The Theban army was renowned for its fighting prowess, and the animosity between the two city states actually led Thebes to forsake its common Greek ancestral ties to Athens and side with the Persian army under Xerxes during the war of 480 BC. Corinth was located strategically on an isthmus that controlled access to both the Ionian and Aegean seas. Corinth was also frequently opposed to Athenian influence and became a prominent naval power in the region. Although the reputation of Corinth was that of a centre of decadence and high living, it was also a commercial hub that generated significant revenue through trade. The influence of Corinth on the development of Greek culture cannot be discounted.

ABOVE: Ruins of ancient Thebes remain to attest to the city state's ancient power. (Creative Commons Davide Mauro via Wikipedia)

View of Corinth.

ABOVE: The ancient city state of Corinth is visible in this engraving from the 19th century. (Public Domain)

ABOVE: Young girls are shown at play in this ancient terra cotta figurine from the city state of Corinth.

(Creative Commons Dosseman via Wikipedia)

ABOVE: This ancient amphora from the city state of Rhodes dates to the 6th century BC.

(Creative Commons George E. Koronaios via Wikipedia)

The growth of the city states inevitably brought them into conflict with one another. Territorial disputes arose from the desire to control neighbouring lands, while the aristocratic ruling classes and well-to-do merchants sometimes quarrelled over favourable trade agreements or divisions of property. From time to time these disagreements erupted into warfare. Throughout the history of ancient Greece, it was not uncommon at any time to have two or more city states at war with one another. At times those city states whose leaders preferred to remain at peace were forced to choose sides for their economic survival. As disputes concerning land ownership and territorial frontiers were common, proliferation of trade made access to the sea essential. Wars were fought over opportunities to exploit the rich natural resources in and around the Peloponnesian and Attic peninsulas, including vast forests of timber, mines that yielded tons of silver, and seas teeming with fish.

At times the city states did find common purpose. They formed the military alliance that defeated the Persian invasion of 480 BC, although this period of cooperation apparently forestalled the internal strife and disagreements that led to the terrible Peloponnesian War several decades later. After Xerxes and the Persians were defeated, Athens, with its superb naval force, became the dominant Greek city state.

The Athenians brought surrounding city states into the Delian League, which in time became more of a protectorate than a cooperative assembly of peers. Some historians even consider the Delian League to be only the façade of a de facto Athenian empire. By the late 5th century BC, however, Sparta had become alarmed by the apparent growth of Athenian influence, and in

431 BC the Peloponnesian War broke out. Corinth had remained a staunch adversary of Athens throughout the turbulent years, and to counter the Delian League, Sparta had assembled the Peloponnesian League.

The devastating war lasted 27 years and ended with Athens defeated. However, an unintended consequence had developed simultaneously. Sparta had been bled white and depleted of resources. Even then in victory, Sparta was too weak to consolidate

its gains, assert authority, assume a viable leadership role, and return the ravaged city states to stability. This unsettled post-war period led to the Theban-Spartan War of 378 BC to 362 BC. Thebes emerged victorious and dominated the Greek world for a brief period.

Again, however, the days of peace were numbered. Philip II, king of Macedonia, became aware of the collective weakness of the city states to the south and invaded from the northeast. His forces defeated the fragile city state alliance led by Athens and Thebes, sealing their fate in conquest at the Battle of Chaeronea in 338 BC.

The story of the Greek city states is perhaps somewhat unique in history. While their relative power and influence waxed and waned, the city states served as the principal exporters of Greek culture and influence throughout the Mediterranean basin. They were dominant in trade and commerce, military might, and in groundbreaking advances in the sciences, philosophy, law, politics, art and government. The city states were, at the same time, quite independent and diverse but very much alike in many respects.

Although there was no doubt that the leaders of the city states recognized one another as Greek, sharing a common heritage, there was continual unrest. They remained fiercely independent of one another, uniting only to meet a major external threat. And then, ironically, they fought one another until all were so weakened that they could no longer fend off an invader intent on conquest.

ABOVE: Columns of the temple of Zeus in Athens retain their ancient grandeur after thousands of years.

(Creative Commons Ustill via Wikipedia)

AGE OF TYRANNY

The increasing stratification of social classes within Greek society gave rise to a greater awareness of political power among the newly affluent of the merchant class and even within the poorer populations of the city states. While the oligarchies of aristocratic leaders had emerged as a means of preventing the rule of an individual monarch, the oligarchies were in turn held with increasing suspicion and mistrust among the people.

The burgeoning class struggle, particularly in the larger city states, sometimes led to the emergence of a "tyrant," broadly defined as a populist politician, as strongman who might bring stability and reform to an increasingly fractious social condition. By definition, the tyrant was a dictator, one whose decisions were above the law, whose actions were not answerable to a governing body, and whose authority was sweeping.

The modern definition of the tyrant bears the connotation of an evil despot, ruling without conscience in a self-serving manner. However, in ancient Greece the tyrant rulers were often moderate and wise. Their authoritarian approach brought about relatively few historic references to cruelty or corruption. The Age of Tyranny is generally accepted as 750 BC to 500 BC, and though some tyrants were deposed, banished, stoned to death, or otherwise assassinated, there were notable exceptions.

The earliest of Greek tyrants came to power from the aristocratic class in an effort to curb the authority of the oligarchies. During the

ABOVE: Solon is depicted in 17th century dress in this period painting. (Public Domain)

course of 250 years, the period of tyrant rule is seen as a bridge from the domination of the aristocratic class to the more representative and democratic forms of government that later took hold within the city states.

Famous tyrants came to power in many city states and left profound impressions on society. In Athens, Draco was the first to place the legal code into writing, establishing the framework as the earliest constitution of the city state. He brought forth a harsh series of laws that required severe punishment for even minor infractions. Introduced in approximately 621 BC, Draco's code came as the people sought social stability; however, it proved to be much sterner than they had expected. The code itself was uniform and presented in the context of formal legal proceedings.

Draco's very name resulted in the modern word "draconian," meaning harsh or severe. The philosopher and historian Plutarch related that the theft of an apple or a head of cabbage was punishable by death. Debtors who defaulted on their payments were subject to enslavement by their creditors. The laws of Draco were said to be written in blood, and he reasoned that petty crimes were deserving of the death penalty while he was unable to find a more suitable punishment for major crimes than death as well. Those who were tried and condemned were put to death in one of three ways, the ingestion of poisonous hemlock, tied to a board and left in the wilderness to starve or

die of exposure, or pitching the guilty into a deep pit or ravine.

Draco's own death is a matter of conjecture. One tale offers that he was so immensely popular that as he entered the theatre on the island of Aegina, the patrons greeted him enthusiastically, tossing their cloaks, hats and shirts over him until he suffocated. He was supposedly buried in the theatre. It is known that Draco was banished from Athens to the island of Aegina and spent many years there until his death at the age of about 50.

Solon is remembered as a lawgiver, who was both a politician and a literary figure. He revised much of the legal system and the constitution, abolishing many of the harsh punishments inherent in Draco's code while dividing Athenian society into four distinct groups, the most affluent known as the pentakosiomedimnoi, followed by the hippeis,

ABOVE: Peisistratus ruled in Athens for 56 years as a good and just tyrant.
(Creative Commons Jean Auguste Dominique Ingres via Wikipedia)

ABOVE: These three men carrying clubs are believed to have been guards for the tyrant Peisistratus.
(Creative Commons Zde via Wikipedia)

ABOVE: Ancient Corinth was the scene of both cruel and benevolent rule under Cypselus. (Public Domain)

zeugitai, and thetes based upon financial capacity. The top three classes to serve as archons in the existing oligarchy. He broadened the participation of the citizenry in Athenian government and politics. Some historians do not classify Solon as a tyrant, given the fact that he championed the lower class and appears to have shunned self-aggrandizement and opportunities for personal gain. He is remembered as one of the Seven Sages of Greece, a group of philosophers and statesmen known for their wisdom.

After Solon, Peisistratus and his sons Hipparchus and Hippias ruled in Athens. Peisistratus reigned for 56 years and gained a reputation as a good and just tyrant. Hipparchus was assassinated several years

later, after dreaming of his own death. Hippias proved a cruel ruler, embittered by his brother's killing, and was later deposed. Cleisthenes, a reformer who furthered participatory government in Athens, came to power in 508 BC and is remembered as the father of Athenian democracy.

Cypselus ruled Corinth for 30 years. He came to power in the 7th century BC after the overthrow of the Bacchiadae, an aristocratic family to which his mother belonged. It was a strange succession in that Herodotus wrote of a warning pronounced by an oracle predicting that dire consequences would befall Corinth if the infant Cypselus was allowed to grow to manhood.

According to Herodotus, the oracle foretold that Cypselus would become a tyrant, prompting the Bacchiadae to plot to kill him in infancy. His mother, however, hid the baby in a chest. Subsequently, the oracle's warning proved accurate. As tyrant, Cypselus was responsible for the banishment of many Corinthians from the city. Herodotus wrote that he ruthlessly "deprived many others of their possessions, but the greatest number by

far were deprived of their lives." Nevertheless, though he was perceived as a demagogue by some, his popularity with the people was extraordinary. He moved with ease through the streets, not requiring a bodyguard because he had no fear of assassination. Cypselus is credited with establishing the tribal system of ancient Corinthian society and accumulating a treasury at Delphi. He was also responsible for Corinthian colonization in northwestern Greece, utilizing the city state's strong fleet to project military strength.

Upon the death of Cypselus in 627 BC, his son, Periander, followed as tyrant and ruled for 40 years. Assessments of Periander's rule are varied. He worked to equitably distribute the wealth of Corinth, and in doing so became an opponent of slaveholders and those who lived lavish lifestyles. He advocated an ambitious building program. He founded the Corinthian colony at Poteidaia and placed his son, Lycophron, in the role of tyrant at the colony of Korkyra. He embarked on a military campaign to conquer the small city of Epidaurus and took his father-in-law, Procles, prisoner. In a fit of rage, he threw his own wife down a flight of stairs, killing her.

Herodotus wrote that Periander was at first a "more gentle" ruler than Cypselus had been. However, he came under the influence of Thrasybulus, tyrant of Miletus, who encouraged him to deal with his wealthy political opponents by murdering them. "It was then that he exhibited every kind of evil to the citizens," the historian wrote. "Periander completed all that Cypselus had left undone in his killing and banishing of Corinthians."

Periander named Lycophron as his successor, but Lycophron was murdered before departing Korkyra in 587 BC to take control of Corinth. According to Herodotus, an oracle had predicted the end of the dynasty with the words, "He and his sons will prosper, but the son of his sons no longer."

Psammetichus, Periander's nephew, acceded to rule for only three years before the Corinthian tyranny faded into history.

ABOVE: Corinthian tyrant Periander was at first benevolent but later cruel. He was assassinated. (Public Domain)

ABOVE: These ruins remain at Poteidaia, a colony authorized by Periander. (Creative Commons Gerhard Haubold via Wikipedia)

ANCIENT GREEK PLACES TO VISIT TODAY

The Greek civilization flourished for centuries in ancient times, and its influence continues to shape the modern world. Long after its cities and colonies have passed into memory, however, the ruins and remnants that remain still conjure the images of grandeur that were uniquely those of antiquity. Greek civilization was emulated by the Romans that followed, and its contributions to government, architecture, literature, science, medicine, and philosophy are incalculable. To see the places where giants of ancient eras lived, the streets they walked, and the mountains they climbed is truly an inspiring experience.

Probably the most recognizable site of Ancient Greek civilization is the Acropolis of Athens. Crowning a hilltop rising 150 metres (490 feet) above the capital city of modern Greece, the Acropolis was an ancient site of learning and political discourse. The term "acropolis" is derived from the Greek phrase "highest point" and is a generic reference to such locations in numerous cities of ancient Greece. Although the Acropolis of Athens was inhabited much earlier, the construction of many of its great structures occurred under Pericles in the 5th century BC. Among the best known ancient buildings in the world, the Parthenon, an grand temple dedicated to Athena, goddess of wisdom, is one of the most prominent features of the Athenian Acropolis, along with the Erechtheion and the Propylaia. The Acropolis of Athens is

ABOVE: The Parthenon stands on the Acropolis of Athens and is one of the most recognizable symbols of ancient Greece. (Creative Commons Steve Swayne via Wikipedia)

one of the most popular sites for visitors in all of Greece, and other ruins, constructed, repaired, and enduring through the centuries, are visible. The view from the summit is worthy of the time invested as well.

The site of the first ancient Olympic games in 776 BC, Olympia was a significant religious sanctuary for ancient Greeks prior to the inaugural athletic contests. The site lies in the northwestern Peloponnese, a considerable distance away from Mount Olympus, the highest peak in Greece and

mythical home of the gods. Olympia was dedicated to the worship of Zeus, king of the gods, probably around the 10th century BC, and its ruins reflect a reverence for the deity, as well as remarkable architecture and engineering skill. Outstanding examples of Greek statuary are visible, including those of Hermes of Praxiteles, Nike of Paionois, and the adornment of the temple of Zeus. The ruins of the stadium where Olympic contests were conducted are visible as well, along with the workshop of the famed sculptor Pheidias, where his impressive work was wrought. The temple of Hera and shrines to other gods and goddesses remain, and more than 70 altars were once active in the worshipful sacrifices that took place. Olympia is approximately 3.5 hours from Athens by car.

The largest Bronze Age archaeological site on the island of Crete is the impressive palace of Knossos. Crete was the nexus of the ancient Minoan society, and Knossos was a population centre as early as the Neolithic period. Archaeological clues indicate that construction of the palace began around 1950 BC, and the building and grounds cover a large three-acre tract. Several phases of construction and renovation occurred through the centuries. Located near the modern city of Heraklion on the northern coast of Crete, the ruins reveal a central courtyard enclosed by

ABOVE: Ruins of the Acropolis of Athens were depicted in this painting from the early 20th century. (Public Domain)

ABOVE: These ruins at Olympia are of the Palestra, a site where ancient wrestling competition occurred.
(Creative Commons John Karakatsanis via Wikipedia)

been damaged, destroyed, and rebuilt on numerous occasions through the centuries. It was dedicated to the god of the sun, music, harmony, light, and healing, and its impressive colonnade has been partially restored to provide visitors with an excellent perspective on the structure in the days of its glory. The temple is located on Mount Parnassus in central Greece and is included in the panhellenic sanctuary of religious structures. The renowned Oracle of Delphi was said to be housed inside the temple. Greek mythology asserts that Apollo slew Python, the menacing dragon that had previously guarded the oracle. Then, after the god became the possessor of the site, he was the object of worship there along with his mother, Leta, and twin sister, Artemis. In Greek tradition, this famed temple is one of five constructed to honour Apollo at the sacred site of Delphi. Modern excavations were begun in 1892, and the priestesses of Apollo, the Pythia, resided there, serving as the actual oracles according to ancient texts.

storage rooms and magazines and a large basin with a holding tank for water that appears to have been used at least initially for religious purposes. The palace appears to have suffered damage through the centuries due to recurring earthquakes and other natural phenomena. Repair and construction work were conducted by the Mycenaeans after their occupation of Crete and absorption of the Minoan territories. A large throne room, central palace sanctuary, and personal quarters have been discovered amid modern excavations. Frescoes, some of which have been restored in modern times, provide vivid decoration.

Southwest of Athens, the ancient theatre of Epidaurus remains resplendent with seating capacity for 14,000 spectators in 55 rows of limestone seats carved into the stone itself in the shape of a bowl for individual comfort. Its advanced acoustics were a technical marvel in ancient times, and visitors can still experience the effects today. Constructed in the late 4th century BC, the ancient theatre is located in the old city of Epidaurus in the southeast section of the sanctuary dedicated to Asclepius, the ancient Greek god of medicine. The architect Polykleitos the Younger designed the theatre, and it is renowned for its beauty and symmetry. The first excavations of the theatre began in the late 1800s, and gradually the classic structure of the Greek theatres has been revealed. The theatre of Epidaurus is built with the theatron, or seating area, along with a skene, a scenic backdrop or wall, and an orchestra, the circular place at the lowest point where the actors and chorus performed. Performances of ancient plays and dramas are still held today in the theatre, and it stands out among other examples of ancient Greek theatre construction because of its acoustics and aesthetics. The theatre is a UNESCO World Heritage site.

Originally constructed in the 4th century BC, the temple of Apollo at Delphi has

ABOVE: The reception courtyard at the Palace of Knossos retains something of its original splendour.
(Creative Commons Dougal96 via Wikipedia)

ABOVE: The theatre of Epidaurus is impressive in its size and technical elements, including superb acoustics.
(Creative Commons Carole Raddato via Wikipedia)

One of the most powerful and influential Greek city states, ancient Corinth is located only 48 miles from Athens. Corinth was known in ancient times as a city of revelry and debauchery. Nevertheless, it possessed a great navy that was at times second only to that of Athens among the city states. Corinth was strategically located halfway between Athens and Sparta and situated on an isthmus, a narrow strip of land that joined the Peloponnesian peninsula to the mainland of Greece. Shards of pottery indicate that the site of Corinth has been inhabited since Neolithic times, approximately 6500 BC. Amid copious ruins from the later Roman era, Corinth includes impressive ruins of temples of Apollo, constructed in the Doric style, and a theatre that was guilt in the 5th century BC. The streets of the old city are visible, coursing alongside the ruins that retain their majesty across time. Corinth was also home to a temple of Aphrodite, and its remnants include fine examples of Greek statuary and sculpture. Archaeological excavations and study at Corinth have been ongoing since 1896, and the city is well known to Christians as the Apostle Paul visited there during his travels across the

ABOVE: The temple of Apollo at Delphi is the legendary home of the ancient oracle. (Creative Commons Helen Simonsson)

Mediterranean and two of his letters to its people are contained in the New Testament.

According to the famed poet Homer, Kamiros, along with Ialyssos and Lindos, was one of the earliest cities on the island of Rhodes that collectively established a major

Greek city state there in the 5th century BC. Founded by the Dorians, there is evidence of a Mycenaean habitation, including a substantial necropolis. The city flourished with an agricultural economy, producing wine, olive oil, and figs, taking full advantage of fertile soil, and was the first city on the island of Rhodes to mint its own coinage. Ruins date back to the 8th century BC, and though the city suffered two devastating earthquakes in antiquity, it is still home to some of the most impressive ruins of the ancient world. Among the ruins that are worthy of exploration are the Doric Fountain House, a covered walkway known as a stoa, and an agora, or marketplace, which was once the bustling centre of trade and commerce for Kamiros. The sanctuary of Athena was built on the acropolis of Kamiros, and only scattered remnants of its original construction are visible, including a deep, rectangular pit that is now surrounded by remains of later construction projects.

The Acropolis of Rhodes is an expansive site that dates back to the 3rd century BC during the Hellenistic period and occupies much of the western portion of the city. Excavations did not begin in earnest there until 1912,

BELOW: The temple of Apollo at Corinth was constructed in the Doric architectural style. (Creative Commons Berthold Werner via Wikipedia)

BOVE: The ruins of the ancient city of Kamiros are located on the island of Rhodes. (Creative Commons Shadowgate via Wikipedia)

ABOVE: The ruins of the temple of Apollo on the Acropolis of Rhodes stand near the sea.

(Creative Commons Jebulon via Wikipedia)

ABOVE: Modern residential structures crowd the temple of Apollo at Syracuse on the island of Sicily. (Creative Commons Laurel Lodged via Wikipedia)

and discoveries include the temple of Pythian Apollo and the Nymphaia, an area originally used for both worship and recreation. The Nymphaia includes four cavernous areas hewn out of the surrounding rock with greenery encircling ancient cisterns and entrance stairs that lead to a large opening in the roof. A stadium, gymnasium, and library are among the functional buildings, as well as the stoa building with its impressive façade. The temple of Athena Polius and Zeus Polius is located in the northern section of the acropolis, and the massive columns and porticos are indicative of Doric architecture. In ancient times, the leaders of Rhodes conducted foreign affairs and treaty related functions there. A significant portion of the Acropolis of Rhodes has yet to be fully excavated, and more wonders are expected to emerge in the future.

Syracuse was one of the most important Greek colonies and developed into a powerful city state in its own right. Located in the southeast of the island of Sicily, it was founded by Corinthian and Tenean settlers and was the home of the eminent mathematician Archimedes. Its archaeological park is a fascinating destination for travellers today, and visitors gain a sense of the perspective of the Roman statesman Cicero, who described Syracuse as "…the greatest Greek city and the most beautiful of them all." Both Greek and Roman ruins are visible in close proximity at Syracuse, and the highlight of the Greek aspect is the theatre constructed in the 5th century BC. The theatre remains remarkably well preserved and appears in much the same condition as it did centuries ago. Its 59 rows of rock seats accommodate up to 15,000 spectators, and it functions today as the host of an annual Greek festival held on the site every spring. The large limestone quarry, located near the theatre, is an interesting site as well. No doubt, stone quarried there was

utilized in building the structures within the archaeological park. A short walk down a scenic path takes visitors to the Ear of Dionysius, a huge cave carved into the side of a hill. Legend has it that Dionysius, once king of ancient Syracuse, used the cave, its entrance shaped like a human ear with excellent acoustics, to eavesdrop on prisoners who were confined nearby.

Ancient Troy plays a pivotal role in the history of Greece and Western civilization. For many years, scientists doubted that the city actually existed. However, in the late 19th century, the German businessman and amateur archaeologist Heinrich Schliemann, enamoured with the history of ancient Greece, endeavoured to locate the city near the town of Hisarlik on the northwest coast of modern Turkey near the Dardanelles, the strait that connects the Black Sea and the Aegean

Sea. Suggestions that Hisarlik might in fact be the site of ancient Troy emerged with Englishman Charles Maclaren in the early 19th century, and Schliemann excavated there in a somewhat haphazard manner between 1870 and 1890. He unearthed evidence of nine separate periods of construction at the site, indicating that successive cities were built and rebuilt, sometime following natural or man-made disasters that caused catastrophic damage to buildings. Available evidence indicates that the area of Troy has been inhabited for nearly 3,000 years. Visitors are greeted by a re-creation of the fabled Trojan Horse and may explore excavations attributed to the Troy of Homer's Iliad, built sometime during the Bronze Age. Believed to be the Troy of Homer's epic poem, the ruins of Troy VI include remnants of thick walls that surrounded the city along with evidence of timbers damaged by flames, suggesting that a great battle took place during the period.

The remains of ancient Greek civilization are scattered across the Mediterranean basin, on the mainland of Greece, the Peloponnesian and Attic peninsulas, and the Greek Isles. Those in search of adventure and intent on gaining a personal perspective on the legacy of ancient Greece will find these sites captivating.

ABOVE: This artist's rendering depicts the reconstruction of a building in ancient Troy.

(Creative Commons Carole Raddato via Wikipedia)

ABOVE: The south gate of ancient Troy is overgrown with vegetation after its excavation years ago.

(Creative Commons Dennis Jarvis via Wikipedia)

BIRTH OF DEMOCRACY

BELOW: This panoramic view of Athens is seen from the Pnyx, where democratic meetings took place. (Creative Commons Tomisti via Wikipedia)

Ancient Athens is revered in modern times as the birthplace of democracy, the basic form of representative government. Actually, Athens was not the sole centre of democratic thought and practice in ancient Greece. Other city states experimented as well. However, Athenian democracy remains the most recognized of Greek adventures in government, and it also provides the best written record of ancient democracy in theory and practice. And by virtue of being the first city state to establish democratic processes, Athens was in fact the cradle of Western democracy as it exists today.

The Athenian concept was a direct democracy, wherein those who were governed and eligible to participate voted directly on matters of justice and law. By the 5th century BC, the population of greater Athens soared to more than 250,000, while its territory extended into the Attic peninsula, requiring the participatory nature of democratic government to extend beyond the boundaries of the core city. Still, all inhabitants of the city state were not full participants, including slaves and non-Athenian residents.

Participants in the Athenian democratic process were first required to demonstrate proof of citizenship. While women were excluded, men over the age of 18 were obliged to attest that their parents were born in Athens and that they were not slaves. So, only an estimated 30,000 to 50,000 residents of Athens are believed to have been eligible to vote on a consistent basis. Further evaluation yields the conclusion that only about 30 per cent of the city state's population was eligible to cast a ballot at any given time.

Athenian democracy was preceded by earlier forms of government that spanned approximately 300 years of civilization. Founded around 900 BC, Athens was first ruled by a monarchy, which at some point extended its authority to a group of noble advisors. Such government lasted approximately a century before the affluent and wealthy, enriched through successful

ABOVE: Visitors explore the summit of the Aeropagus, a meeting place of affluent Athenians during the democratic period. (Creative Commons George E. Koronaios via Wikipedia)

ABOVE: The rocky hill of the Aeropagus rises 115 metres west of the Acropolis in Athens.
(Creative Commons Ken Russell Salvador via Wikipedia)

ABOVE: A hearing is conducted during a meeting of the Aeropagus in Athens. (Creative Commons Rogers Fund, 1961 via Wikipedia)

business ventures, began to assert their own political views.

Seeking a voice in their own government, influential noblemen began meeting regularly at a familiar hill in Athens called the Aeropagus. They adopted its name as their own, and the Aeropagus flexed its political muscle with the election of nine rulers, known as Archons. The Archons ruled as an oligarchy, but their authority was not absolute. Their decisions required the approval of the full Aeropagus, which at times sparked lively debate.

By 650 BC, the Athenian social structure had become more pronounced, and the wealthy continued to dominate local politics. The ruling class and the Aeropagus itself began to feel the growing discontent with the existing system of government as the working class and poorer elements of Athens resented the total domination of the affluent. In fact, some critics perceived that the wealthy maintained and expanded their affluence through the direct exploitation of the lower classes.

Wealth and family bloodlines were shunted aside as the "tyrants" came to power in most of the Greek city states. Initially, the tyrants were endorsed by the masses and swept into government on the strength of promises to restore stability amid the upheaval of civil strife. The tyrants were not usually cruel or treacherous individuals, as the name "tyrant" is interpreted today, but often thoughtful, well-meaning and talented individuals.

Draco, known as the first legislator of record in ancient Athens, introduced a written legal code in approximately 621 BC. Prior to the code, oral and tribal law had been passed down through generations of Athenians. The code was more uniform and consistent than the previous practice and intended for interpretation within the framework of a court of law. The code itself specified

ABOVE: Solon is depicted as the wise lawgiver of Athens. (Public Domain)

severe penalties, even for minor infractions, and its author's name brought the adjective "draconian" into modern language.

The first written constitution of Athens, Draco's code was prepared at the behest of the people; however, they did not realize in the beginning just how harsh it would be. When Draco was once questioned as to his specification of a death sentence for the guilty in so many circumstances of minor criminal activity, he replied that those who had been convicted were deserving of death and that he could conceive of no harsher punishment for those guilty of major crimes. The code is also believed to have favoured the nobility over the lower classes and was, therefore, inherently flawed.

Draco is believed to have been a nobleman from somewhere on the Attic peninsula.

Born around 650 BC, he died at the age of roughly 50, and for reasons that are unknown he was banished from Athens to the island of Aegina, where he spent many years of his life.

Democracy began to take hold after Solon, an Archon, statesman and poet of good reputation, came to power in 594 BC. Some historians have described Solon as one of the so-called tyrants, while others have set him apart, viewing Solon's rule as distinctive. Regardless, he initiated governmental reform that elevated the participation of the average Athenian citizen in government amid difficult economic times.

Experiencing financial hardship, many citizens of Athens were compelled to prevail on the aristocracy for help. In exchange for loan proceeds, they were regularly required to mortgage their farms and land holdings or even offer themselves or other family members as indentured servants in the event of default – literally as human collateral. If a debt could not be retired according to the terms of the contract, families were routinely relegated to voluntary servitude, slaves to their wealthy masters. An indefinite continuation of the process would lead to financial catastrophe and threaten the foundations of Athenian economic and social stability.

Solon, therefore, became determined to redefine the social structure of Athens, pivoting away from the existing condition that relied on wealth alone. He authored a constitution that separated Athenian society into four classes relative to financial position and allowing the three upper classes to serve as Archons. Solon abolished the custom of securing loans with collateral that involved the potential forfeiture of a person's freedom. His constitution further provided all Athenians with the right to appeal a legal decision to a jury of citizens, effectively curbing the authority of the nine Archons with a larger body, more representative of the general population of the city state.

ABOVE: Cleisthenes is remembered as the father of Athenian democracy. (Attribution ohiostatehouse.org via Wikipedi

The constitution allowed all Athenian citizens to vote for individuals among a slate of candidates for the post of Archon. From those chosen candidates, nine individuals were chosen by lot to fill the positions. A council of 400 citizens formed a representative assembly, and the Aeropagus was given responsibility for the maintenance and upkeep of the law. Although he did not thoroughly eliminate the oligarchy, Solon established aspects of the more complete democracy that would emerge in later years.

Solon remains an example of the public servant. Born into an aristocratic family and likely given the option to pursue a more comfortable existence, he chose to become a spokesman and political champion for the rights of the lower classes. To demonstrate his sincere belief in the reforms and dispel any notion that he somehow intended to take full power for himself, Solon stipulated that Athens should govern itself under the terms of the constitutional model for a decade and then departed from the city state for an extended period of time.

Athenian democracy grew in stature and practice through the early 6th century BC, when an ironic set of circumstances that on the surface appeared to threaten its existence actually strengthened its place in society. During the rule of the tyrant Peisistratus and his sons, Hippias and Hipparchus, an army of mercenaries was always ready to enforce the tyrants' will. However, at the same time Peisistratus was an advocate for the expansion of some institutions sponsored by Solon, even further weakening the influence of the aristocracy and redistributing some lands on the Attic peninsula to stimulate agriculture and develop profitable trade. Half a century under the father and sons ended in 510 BC when the aristocratic Alcmeonidae family deposed Hippias with the help of a Spartan army.

ABOVE: Solon is depicted as a ruler in this painting from the 17th century. (Public Domain)

ABOVE: The speaker's platform in the Pnyx is a reminder of the location where Athenian democracy was practiced. (Creative Commons author unknown via Wikipedia)

BOVE: Pericles succeeded Ephialtes and became first itizen of Athens. (Creative Commons Marie-Lan Nguyen via Wikipedia)

A brief power struggle followed, and in 508 BC Isagoras was elected an Archon. However, Cleisthenes, his rival and a member of the Alcmeonidae family, appealed to the lower classes of Athenians in his own bid for power. Isagoras once again called on a Spartan army to help maintain his rule, but a popular uprising in favour of Cleisthenes led to the summary ejection of Isagoras and the Spartans from Athens.

Cleisthenes dealt with the issue of social class with a seismic shift, and with his leadership Athenian democracy flourished. He is remembered truly as the father of the political movement, though his rule was brief, from only 508 BC to 502 BC. Effectively, Cleisthenes removed the barriers of social class based upon wealth with reforms that provided a new perspective among Athenians. Previously the citizenry had identified themselves as individuals from certain families, but under Cleisthenes they were encouraged to call themselves by names associated with their home villages. The village, therefore, became the basic

political unit of the reshaped society and was known as the "deme." Redirecting identities from family lineage to geographic location fostered an "Athenian identity" rather than a link through bloodline and proved effective in suppressing another potential tyrant who might rise up to challenge the status quo.

With the reshaping of society, each deme was under the direct administration of a demarch, who functioned basically as a town mayor. His responsibilities included categorizing the residents into three groups known as "thirds." These included males who were over 18 and therefore citizens, citizens selected to serve on the local council, and those citizens who were eligible to serve in the assembly. Cleisthenes more fully engaged Athenians in the governmental process by abolishing the old tribal system with a new structure. Ten new tribes were created, and each "third" was assigned to one of these. Then, within each tribe were three thirds, one from the interior of the city state, one from the city itself, and one from the nearby coastal region. Finally, each tribe annually

ABOVE: Bronze voting discs such as these were used in ancient Athens. (Creative Commons C. de Lisle via Wikipedia)

sent a delegation of 50 citizens to serve on a newly expanded council of 500, with 20 percent more overall representation than the early council of 400 under Solon.

Giving a nod to tradition and historical context as well as to provide legitimacy to his new social order, Cleisthenes named each of the 10 tribes after one of the city states heroes from antiquity. These names, he offered, were given to the people by the sun god, Apollo, through the Oracle of Delphi, and the roster included Ajax, Aegeus, Acamas, Antiochus, Erechtheus, Hippothoon, Cecrops, Leos, Oeneus, and Pandion. The tribes' namesakes were revered and given the honour of a statue placed in the agora of Athens for public view near the area of the marketplace where new proclamations and laws were publicly displayed.

Cleisthenes brilliantly strove to minimize the possibility of regional or provincial politics undermining the process in the future. He ordered that once a citizen was registered with a particular village, he remained with that village as a governmental participant regardless of whether he relocated to another region of the city state. The structure succeeded in bringing citizens from all areas of Athens together. With the citizenry thoroughly engaged in self-government even to the local level, the

10 tribes became quite influential in the burgeoning democratic process.

Calling his new form of government demokratia, or rule by the people, Cleisthenes implemented a basic structure of three salient pillars, the maintenance of equity, dispensing of justice, and the writing and interpretation of the law. In practical application, Athenian democracy has been described as a rather boisterous, litigious, and raucous institution. Remarkably, though, it was responsible for a fundamental revision of the role of government in the lives of the people and their ability to chart the course of future events. One of the most significant events in the history of the Western world, the emergence of Athenian democracy was flawed in its denial of full participation to many residents. Still, the century of its maturing, from Solon to Cleisthenes, was a logical progression from the foundation of the former to the flowering and nurture of the latter.

The central governing authority in Athens was the assembly, or ekklesia. During its earliest period, the ekklesia met only 10 times per year, but gradually that number was expanded to 40 annual meetings while called meetings were also held as needed. Any citizen of Athens was free to attend the meetings, and they were held in an open theatre called Pnyx just west of the Acropolis. The revision of existing laws and authoring of new measures were primary responsibilities, while the ekklesia also held public officials accountable in the event of misconduct, deliberated foreign policy issues, and debated whether or not the city state should go to war. Gatherings were often substantial with as many as 5,000 in attendance, although commitments to military service, the harvest season, or other responsibilities curbed the number of spectators at times.

Adult male Athenians considered it their duty to attend meetings of the ekklesia, and indeed at some gatherings attendance was required. An air of formality pervaded the proceedings as slaves extended a rope that was stained red across the agora to funnel the citizenry into the theatre, and those who wore clothing streaked with the red stain

ABOVE: The kleroterion was a device used in the selection process of individuals for service in the juries of ancient Athens. (Creative Commons Marsyas via Wikipedia)

were assessed a fine. Those citizens attending the ekklesia were paid for their time beginning in the late 5th century, but only the first 6,000 received the monetary stipend while the red rope, watched closely, was used to prevent late arrivals from discreetly mixing into the crowd.

The council of 500 was known as the boule, and each of the 50 individuals chosen from the 10 tribes served a term of one year. The boule met daily, and its responsibility was broad, from dealing with the emissaries from other city states or foreign realms to the disposition of livestock and ships' cargoes. Therefore, the actions of the boule were tremendously influential on the daily lives of Athenians. The boule also acted as a body to determine those issues presented before it that were worthy of further presentation to the ekklesia. Such a gatekeeper function gave the boule significant authority in the democratic process.

One interesting component regarding the formation of the boule emanated from a general perspective on elections. The Athenians reasoned that elections were subject to bribery, back room deal brokering, and outside influence. They were corruptible and might allow an individual to maintain a seat in the boule for years, establishing a perpetual class of career officials tempted by the lure of personal gain or financial enhancement. Therefore, seats in the boule were determined by lot. Those whose names were drawn were simply lucky. The lottery approach would hopefully ensure against corruption. However, historians have come across evidence that certain individuals and members of certain families seemed to serve with regularity, much more so than others. That begs the question as to whether the lotteries were completely free of chicanery.

Another essential component of Athenian democracy was the court system, or dikasteria, which was a model of form and function. Every day, a pool of eligible males over 30 years of age was assembled. From among them 500 jurors were chosen by lot. These jurors heard cases that were brought to court directly by the people in the absence of a police force that arrested accused criminals and held them for trial or a process that summoned civil defendants to appear. There was no formal "charge" read against a defendant, so the jury heard the particulars of a case and exercised tremendous authorit

ABOVE: The ruins of the Deme of Koile are reminders of the great reorganization of ancient Athenian society. (Creative Commons Schuppi via Wikipedia)

ABOVE: An archer watches over citizens of Athens as they cast their votes in this pottery image. (Public Domain)

in the disposition of it, as fellow citizens argued for and against one another.

Prosecutors and defendants did argue cases, with the accuser taking centre stage first. A water clock noted the passage of time as each participant was allotted a single speech with duration no longer than three hours. Private cases involved restricted time allotments. Contrary to modern practice, jurors were known to commonly shout their approval of a certain point or to express their displeasure with another. The atmosphere of the courtroom was often boisterous and a bit chaotic, but a case was not allowed to linger more than a day without a decision. After opposing arguments were concluded, there was no specific time allowed for jury deliberations. The case was handed to the jurors, minimal discussion occurred, and a verdict was pronounced.

Cases of all kinds found their way into the Athenian court, and there were no real prohibitions regarding the reason for litigation. Adversaries sometimes had one another brought to court simply for the opportunity to openly ridicule or exact vengeance against their enemy. Interestingly, jurors were expected to render a decision on the motivation of an accuser as well as the culpability of a defendant. In 462 BC, jurors began receiving pay for their service, and this was done logically with the expectation that jury duty would be something all eligible Athenians would want to participate in. The privilege of jury service was not to be reserved for the wealthy or those who could afford to lose a day's wages while away from their jobs.

An early leader of the democratic movement in Athens, Ephialtes began to use the courts about this same time in an effort to further diminish the influence of the Aeropagus. He succeeded in stripping much of its original power away and vesting it in the ekklesia, dikasteria, or boule, while also prosecuting members of the Aeropagus for discharging their duties in a poor or inefficient manner, thus discrediting the body's worth. At long last, Ephialtes reduced the Aeropagus from its status as the guardian of the constitution to its own court, which judged cases of murder and those related to religious practices.

Ephialtes paid for his reforms with his life. He was assassinated in 461 BC, probably at the direction of angered members of

the Aeropagus. His deputy, Pericles, then became a prominent and powerful Athenian. Controversy surrounds the conduct of Pericles, whose influence became so great that he was referred to as the "first citizen of Athens." Historians debate whether Pericles advanced democracy through efforts to improve the lot of the lower classes or whether his personal power overshadowed and impeded the function of the Athenian government.

Despite the upheaval of the Peloponnesian War and the brief reinstatement of an oligarchy in 411 BC, democratic ideals and practices endured for many years in Athens. The Spartans won a military victory over Athens in 404 BC, and the one-year rule of the Thirty Tyrants was quickly followed by the return of democracy. In 338 BC, however, King Philip II and the Macedonian army conquered most of Greece and ended the great Athenian democratic experience.

While its tenure may have been somewhat short given the expansive history of ancient

ABOVE: This inscription lists the names of Athenian citizens chosen as archons for a particular year. (Creative Commons Furius via Wikipedia)

Greece, principles of Athenian democracy survived to influence the Roman republic that followed and amazingly to provide a template for modern democratic government.

ABOVE: The image of the goddess Athena symbolizes democracy. This statue stands before the Austrian parliament house. (Public Domain)

THE HOPLITE

For centuries, the Greek soldier was known as the hoplite, a heavy infantryman. The hoplites were not professional soldiers, but rather members of the wealthy and upper middle classes or landowners who had civilian vocations. The individual was required to pay for his own weapons and equipment, and the sheer cost may well have prevented some who were willing from actually entering service.

The primary fighting formation of the Greek armies was the phalanx, which was usually eight hoplites deep with a broad front that might extend to 100 men or more. The soldiers became adept at locking their shields together to provide mutual protection and extended their spears through it. As opposing phalanxes closed for battle, the rear rank exerted tremendous pressure toward the front. When one phalanx or the other was compromised, its hoplites usually made a hasty retreat.

The hoplite carried a heavy wooden shield with a bronze veneer called a hoplon. It weighed between eight and 15 kilograms (17.64 to 33 pounds), and though it appeared to be somewhat unwieldy, it was quite effective in the heat of battle and facilitated the formation of the phalanx. The hoplite rested a portion of the shield on his shoulder, bearing much of the weight and allowing him to slide his shield into that of the adjacent soldier.

The hoplite was outfitted with heavy armour that is believed to have weighed as much as 31.75 kilograms (70 pounds), including a chest plate called a curaiss that was secured to his body with a system of leather thongs. He wore a tall bronze helmet and shin guards called greaves that protected the legs to the front.

His primary weapon was the doru, a spear with a sharp tip of bronze or later iron with a full length of nearly three metres (9.84 feet). The shaft of the doru was wooden, and the butt sometimes was fitted with an iron spike called a sauroter, which literally translates into English as "lizard killer." The sauroter could be driven into the ground to provide stability in defensive positions or turned toward the enemy in close-quarter combat.

When opposing armies clashed and the doru was expended or lost, the hoplite had a secondary weapon that he was often highly trained to utilize. A short sword called a xiphos, roughly .65 metres (2.6 feet) long and sporting a curved, double-edged blade that resembled the shape of a leaf, was ideal for thrusting and hacking. When Macedonian troops under Alexander the Great mounted military expeditions in the 4th century BC, they brought with them a longer spear called the surissa, which extended up to five metres (16.4 feet). Light infantrymen called psiloi provided support for the hoplites in battle, carrying slings and stones, as well as javelins.

Armies of ancient Greece included cavalry formations that were populated by accomplished horsemen usually of the upper classes. Again, the cavalry soldier was responsible for the cost of his mount and his arms and equipment, which would have been prohibitive for those of the lower classes. Cavalry played a more prominent role as warfare progressed, and by the Peloponnesian War its numbers were significant, even though the phalanx still dominated the land battle. The Macedonian armies of King Philip II and Alexander the Great utilized cavalry more liberally than their predecessors, recognizing the advantages of speed, mobility, and scouting that their horsemen provided. The rapid movement of cavalry formations, sweeping around the enemy flank to complete an envelopment, hastened the demise of the hoplite era.

ABOVE: Two hoplites are shown in attack positions with weapons and shields. (Public Domain)

ABOVE: Hoplites go into battle as musicians play in the decorative motif of this vase. (Public Domain)

ABOVE: A Greek hoplite of the 5th century BC is shown with shield and spear. (Creative Commons Jona Lendering via Wikipedia)

THE MESSENIAN WARS

The story of the Messenian Wars provides an excellent illustration of the rivalries that existed among the city states of Greece, which lingered throughout their existence. Sparta and Messenia were city states that existed in close territorial proximity to one another. Although they shared a common heritage, there were differences that bred animosity.

The Spartans were of Dorian ancestry and moved into the northern Peloponnesian peninsula around 1100 BC, taking significant territory from the Achaeans, another of the four major tribes that inhabited greater Greece according to the ancient historian Herodotus. The other three were the Dorians, Aeolians, and Ionians.

Along with the Spartan invasion from the southern Balkans, some of their number settled in areas already populated by Achaeans, and inevitably over time these Spartan transplants developed a more distinctive society as they absorbed Achaean customs and practices. Cultural ties between the Achaeans and their Spartan cousins began to fray over time, and competition for natural resources emerged. Both contributed to a rather volatile relationship that overflowed into armed conflict around 743 BC. The first Messenian War lasted a full 20 years before peace was achieved with the Spartan victory. Two more wars later erupted, the Second Messenian War of 660 BC to 650 BC, and the Third Messenian War of the mid-5th century BC. The second and

ABOVE: This ancient amphitheatre is located in Messenia, a land conquered by the Spartans.
(Creative Commons Herbert Ortner via Wikipedia)

ABOVE: This example of an ancient Greek burial chamber is located in Messenia. (Creative Commons Puelle via Wikipedia)

third wars were both sparked by uprisings among the helots, a large population of Messenia and neighbouring Laconia who were enslaved by the Spartans for an extended period.

Animosity had smouldered for some time, especially following Messenian harassment of Spartan maidens in the temple of Artemis Limnatis during a religious ritual. Some historians believe that the so-called maidens were actually Spartan soldiers in disguise, violating the spirit of the sanctuary. The temple is believed to have been destroyed, but a declared war did not break out for another 25 years.

The proximate cause of the First Messenian War was the theft of cattle. Some accounts relate that a Messenian Olympic champion, Polychares of Messenia, had helped himself to the cattle, sparking numerous retaliatory raids by the Spartans who inflicted significant damage and caused casualties. Others, however, relate that the cattle belonged to the Olympian and grazed on land that he leased from Euaiphnos, a Spartan. Deceitfully, Euaiphnos sold the cattle to merchants and lied to their owner, telling him that pirates had stolen the animals.

When a servant of Polychares escaped from the merchants and returned to tell his master the true facts of the story, Euaiphnos confessed and asked Polychares to allow his son to go with him to collect the money from the sale. Instead, Euaiphnos murdered the son as soon as he had crossed the border

into Sparta. Polychares asked Spartan magistrates for justice but feared he would not be treated equitably in a foreign legal action. Therefore, he began to randomly murder any Spartan he came across. Both governments demanded the extradition of the accused men to the other for prosecution. Subsequently, the incident sparked all-out war; the legal case was apparently lost in the confusion.

Still, other historians speculate that the reason for the war was Spartan expansionism. In truth, the separation of fact

ABOVE: This bust of Artemis, Greek goddess of the hunt and twin sister of Apollo, is now housed in a museum in Italy. (Creative Commons Marie-Lan Nguyen via Wikipedia)

ABOVE: This modern view of Messenia is seen from the summit of Mount Ithome.
(Creative Commons Stefan Artinger via Wikipedia)

ABOVE: Ancient ruins remain at the base of Mount Ithome in Messenia. (Creative Commons Stafan Artinger via Wikipedia)

from fiction is difficult during this ancient period, and it is likely that Spartan territorial ambitions were responsible.

Regardless, the Spartans did actually invade Messenia. King Alcmenes commanded the invading army, marching on the city of Ampheia under cover of darkness. Arriving at Ampheia, the Spartans surprised the city, slaughtering the adult males they encountered and enslaving the women and children.

In response, King Euphaes of Messenia raised an army, which fought a number of inconclusive engagements against the invaders. Each side continually raided across the borders in to the other as well, and after several years of campaigning occurred, Alcemenes died and was succeeded by his son, Polydorus. While a Spartan army marched westward, Cleonnis led a Messenian army eastward to engage in a major battle.

The two armies clashed on the plain near the mountains of Taygetus, the exact location unknown, and fought an inconclusive battle. The heavy infantry of the two sides fought with desperation, the Spartans said to have used the phalanx, although there is no evidence that the battlefield formation was in use by them at the time. The historian Pausanius described

the fight, relating that the Messenians "… ran charging… reckless with their lives… Some of them leaped out of rank and did glorious deeds of courage." The Spartans, however, "were careful not to break ranks… knowledge of war was something they had been brought up to… they kept a deeper formation, expecting the Messenians not to hold a line against them for as long as their own would hold…"

The First Messenian War continued for 20 years, and after a brutal battle near the previously destroyed city of Ampheia, where neither side showed mercy to the other, the Messenians were compelled to retreat. They fortified a position on the high ground of Mount Ithome, towering 800 metres (2,400 feet), and assumed a defensive posture. The Messenians then consulted the Oracle of Delphi for guidance as the war entered its second decade. The oracle advised them to sacrifice a royal

virgin, and the daughter of Aristodemus, a nobleman who may in fact have succeeded Euphaes as king, was chosen.

When the Spartans received word of the sacrifice, they refrained from a major attack on the defences at Mount Ithome for several years. Then, the Spartans consulted the Oracle of Delphi as well. There is no record of the instructions given to them; however, the Messenians were probably strangled by a protracted siege, which led Aristodemus to commit suicide just as Mount Ithome fell to the Spartans. Many Messenians were killed or fled, while many more were captured and enslaved.

The Spartan victory in the First Messenian War brought wealth and land to the city state, supporting the further rise of the warrior class and the building of a formidable military power. The remaining Messenians were enslaved, their social class becoming known as the helots. The captivity was harsh, and the helots endured until a poet named Tyrtaeus fomented a rebellion that led to the Second Messenian War of the mid-7th century. The conflict lasted a decade before the uprising was quelled, and the constant unrest was probably responsible in part for the further development of militarism in Sparta.

The Messenians rose once more in 464 BC, stubbornly holding out again on Mount Ithome until they were finally allowed to leave Messenia. Some of the former slaves settled in Sicily, while others moved into central Greece and occupied territory near the city of Naupactus.

While the First Messenian War and its two subsequent conflicts are among the lesser-known wars of antiquity, their impact on history remains substantial. The city state of Sparta known for its militarism, discipline, and devotion to the dominion as a whole rather than the individual, might not have developed as it did otherwise.

ABOVE: This engraving depicts the powerful Greek city state of Sparta. (Public Domain)

THE FIRST PERSIAN WAR

One of the most distinctive features of the Greek city states was their independence. They were so bent on remaining autonomous that they often went to war with one another if they felt a threat to that status. However, when an outside menace surfaced, the city states did call upon one another for assistance.

Such was the case with the First Persian War, which pitted the city states of Athens and Eritrea against the colossus of the Persian Empire, the great enemy to the east ruled by King Darius I, otherwise known as Darius the Great. In the early 5th century BC, the Persian Empire was in its youth, and its ruler remained intent on expansion. Darius had seized the throne previously and had been distracted by continual uprisings at home; however, his desire to expand the empire had not been dissuaded.

Darius had sent military expeditions into the interior of Europe, as far to the north and west as the River Danube. His army had conquered Thrace, a large territory in eastern Europe encompassing modern Bulgaria, eastern mainland Greece, and western Turkey. The Persians conquered the Paeonians of northern Macedonia and compelled Macedonia proper to become a puppet client state. The Persians and the city states of ancient Greece had been on a collision course for some time, particularly after Darius and his legions conquered the city states of Ionia, a region on the western coast of Asia Minor, now in modern Turkey. The Ionian city states were originally settled by Athenians, which presented a traditional link between the peoples that ran deeper than simple Greek association.

ABOVE: Persian King Darius I vowed to subjugate the Athenias and Eretrians. (Creative Commons Surenae via Wikipedia)

RIGHT: Persian warriors are depicted in this frieze from the palace of Darius I at Susa. (Public Domain)

Surely, the Persians understood that their course of conquest would bring them into open conflict with the Greek city states to the west, while the Greeks of Athens, Eritrea, and other city states recognized the real threat to their sovereignty that the aggressive Persians posed.

In 500 BC, the Ionian Greeks rose up against their Persian masters, and the insurrection grew so intense that it threatened the stability of the entire Persian Empire, siphoning away military assets from other areas of the dominion and placing further territorial expeditions on hold. The

Ionian revolt had begun when the Persian satrap Artaphernes and the tyrant Aristagoras of the city state of Miletus had mounted a joint campaign against the island of Naxos. When the campaign failed, the relationship between the two leaders soured. Artaphernes intended to remove Aristagoras from power in Miletus, but Aristagoras moved first, resigning as tyrant and declaring Miletus a democracy. Other Ionian city states under the Persian heel seized the opportunity, removed their Persian appointed tyrants, and declared themselves democracies as well.

As the rebellion widened, the Ionians called upon their fellow Greeks to rally to their aid. Only Athens and Eritrea responded to the call. The involvement of Athens was the culmination of festering animosity between the Athenians and the Persians that dated back to 510 BC as the Athenian democracy was emerging. In that year, the Athenians had removed the tyrant Hippias, the last member of the family of Peisistratus that had ruled for 36 of the last 50 years, from power. With the aid of the Persians, Hippias found sanctuary at the court of Artaphernes and promised Athenian servitude to the Persians in exchange for assistance in regaining power.

Cleisthenes proposed democratic rule in Athens as an alternative to a pro-Sparta regime under the tyrant Isagoras. However, Isagoras banished Cleisthenese from the city. At this time, the Athenian people clamoured for democracy and actually removed Isagoras, restoring Cleisthenes. The grip of democracy on the collective psyche of the Athenians hardened them even further to the return of the

ABOVE: King Darius I tramples a rival under his feet in this relief. (Creative Commons Leen van Dorp via Wikipedia)

ABOVE: A Greek hoplite and Persian warrior do battle in this image created in the 5th century BC. (Public Domain)

tyrant Hippias. The Spartans were not finished yet, and a Spartan army, led by Cleomenes, marched on Athens. This expedition ended in failure, but not before the Athenians had petitioned Artaphernes for assistance.

Artaphernes instructed the Athenian emissaries to present him with earth and water, traditional signs of submission. They agreed but were severely criticized for the gesture when they returned to Athens. When Cleomenes failed to restore Hippias to power, the latter again fled to Artaphernes and his capital city of Sardis. Attempting to dissuade direct Persian interference in their affairs, the Athenians sent ambassadors to Sardis again. Artaphernes told them flatly to return Hippias to power. They refused, becoming the sworn enemies of the Persians.

When the Ionians appealed for military aid, Athens was already deeply invested in the outcome of the revolt. The Eretreans probably entered the war against Persia to protect their trade routes along the Aegean Sea, which would likely have been lost with Persian domination of the eastern Mediterranean. The specific reasons for Eretrean involvement, however, have actually been lost to history.

In 498 BC, a combined force of 25 Athenian and Eretrean triremes, the warships of the day, sailed for Sardis. The attackers outmanoeuvred the Persians and set fire to much of the city. However, that was the high water mark of the expedition. Soon enough, Persian forces counterattacked, and their superb cavalry pushed the Greeks back to the coast. Subsequently, the Persians won a significant victory in the naval Battle of Lade in 494 BC, and the insurrection petered out after six years of fighting. The Persians then extended their empire northward to the Sea of Marmara and eastward, seizing islands in the Aegean. Darius I, his anger burning furiously, was determined then to exact revenge against Athens and Eritrea, whose interference on the side of the Ionians had now provided a pretext for military action that he believed would make the Persians masters of all of Greece.

By the spring of 492 BC, the Persians were ready to advance against the Greeks. An invasion force on both land and sea was commanded by Mardonius, the king's son-in-law. The Persian army marched through Ionia, and in an effort to prevent an uprising Mardonius ironically deposed the tyrant rulers and installed democratic governments among the city states. The Persians reasserted control in Thrace and then fully subjugated Macedonia. The Persian fleet departed for the northern Aegean, reached the Greek islands, and began to skirt the Greek coastline around Acanthus. However, as the ships reached the coast near Mount Athos, a tremendous storm wreaked havoc. According to the Greek historian Herodotus, whose amalgamation of fact and fiction serves as the principal account of the First Persian War, the Persians lost 20,000 men and 300 ships, effectively shattering the seaborne threat to the Greeks.

More catastrophe followed as the Persian army's camp in Macedonia was attacked by warriors of a local Thracian tribe called the Brygians. The attackers fell on the camp under cover of darkness, wounding Mardonius and killing many Persian soldiers. Nevertheless, the Persians rallied and defeated the Brygians. Still, the army under Mardonius was too weak to fight the Greeks. Both the army and the navy retired after this great exercise in futility. The only significant accomplishment of the first campaign had been the securing of approaches to Greece for a second military expedition.

Darius I was far from finished, determined to punish the Athenians and Eritreans, and the Greeks were well aware of the danger that had only temporarily subsided. Always cunning, Darius then decided to take a diplomatic approach. He sent envoys to the Greek city states asking them to submit by presenting earth and water as signs of fealty. Many Greek leaders were cowed by the underlying threat of Persian military strength. The Athenians, though, arrested the envoys, put them on trial, and then executed them to a man. The Spartans unceremoniously threw the Persian

ABOVE: Persian King Darius I failed in his attempt to conquer Greece beyond the colonies of Ionia. (Creative Commons Carlo Raso via Wikipedia)

ambassadors sent to their court down a deep well. In doing so, the Spartans cast their lot with Athens in the fighting to come, but a wave of internal discord slowed their military involvement.

Aware of the difficulties in Sparta, Darius moved forward with his second military action, hoping to defeat the Athenians and their allies, the Plataeans, while Sparta was distracted. He assembled a new invasion fleet, and historians estimate its immensity as approximately 600 triremes and as many as 300,000 to 600,000 infantry and cavalry. Darius placed Datis and Artaphernes, the son of the satrap, in command of the huge force, ordering an amphibious attack against the Athenians.

When the Persian fleet sailed from Cilicia, its first objective was the city of Lindos on the island of Rhodes. That siege was said to have been unsuccessful with the Persian fleet sailing along the coast of Asia Minor to Naxos, where revenge was exacted for interference with the earlier Persian expedition. The city of Naxos was burned

ABOVE: Persians and Greeks engage in combat in this image from the First Persian War. (Creative Commons Carlo Raso via Wikipedia)

ABOVE: Persian naval forces used triremes such as this during their ill-fated expedition to Greece.
(Creative Commons OmicronR via Wikipedia)

ABOVE: Persian refugees flee Sardis, burned by the Athenians and Eretrians in support of Ionia. (Public Domain)

to the ground, and those who did not flee to the surrounding mountains were sent into slavery. However, Datis chose leniency for the populations of other islands if they submitted. The Persians moved on to the Cyclades, a cluster of islands in the Aegean. At Delos, he offered homage to the gods of the island before sailing further across the sea. Other islands were not so fortunate when they did not readily comply with Datis's demands. Hostages were taken, and citizens were impressed into the Persian force on several occasions before its arrival at the island of Euboea. There, the inhabitants of the coastal town of Karystos refused at first to supply hostages but bowed to Persian demands when their town was besieged and the surrounding countryside devastated.

Sailing around Euboea, the Persians approached Eretria, the initial objective of the expedition. Lively debate took place among the Eretreans as they became aware of the approaching Persian host. Options were limited to full-scale evacuation, bowing to the Persians, or accepting the difficulties of a potentially protracted siege. The leaders chose to allow the Persians to besiege their city and made no attempt to give battle in the open.

The Persians marched from the shore an attacked the city for six days without making any substantial gains as both sides suffered heavy casualties. On the seventh day, a pair of treacherous Eretreans betrayed their countrymen and opened the gates of the city, allowing the marauding Persians to enter and sow destruction. The city was burned and looted, while the surviving Eretreans were enslaved.

Flush with victory, the Persians sailed further along the Attic peninsula, arriving in the bay of Marathon. Hippias, the deposed tyrant of Athens, advised Datis to land and advance to the plain of Marathon, only 40 kilometres (25 miles) from Athens.

The Persians came ashore in full view of the Athenians and Plataeans. A few days later, they divided their forces, intending to fight the Athenian army at Marathon with one force while the other Persian detachment would fall upon the lightly defended city of Athens.

The ensuing Battle of Marathon was one of the most pivotal engagements in Western history. The Athenian victory temporarily preserved Greek and Western culture. When the subsequent Persian attempt to take Athens was thwarted, the invaders had no choice but to turn their triremes toward home in defeat.

ABOVE: Eretria stood with Athens against the invasion of the Persians following the Ionian Revolt. (Creative Commons George E. Koronalos via Wikipedia)

THE BATTLE OF MARATHON

ABOVE: Greek hoplites rush forward against the Persians at the Battle of Marathon in this 1859 painting by Georges Richegrosse. (Public Domain)

Significantly outnumbered, the Athenians, under Miltiades, chose to meet the Persians on the plain of Marathon on September 10, 490 BC. It was a departure from previous battles since Greek forces had chosen to defend from within their city walls rather than risk a fight in the open. According to Herodotus, the Greeks had never been able to even hold their line intact when fighting the Persians.

As the Athenians watched the Persians flood the plain, they appealed to Sparta for assistance. Miltiades despatched his swiftest runner, Pheidippides, to cover 150 miles to the distant city with a message. "Men of Sparta," read the plea, "the Athenians ask you to help them and not stand by while the most ancient city of Greece is crushed and enslaved by a foreign invader. Already Eretria is destroyed and her people in chains, and Greece is weaker by the loss of one fine city."

According to Herodotus, the Spartans were sympathetic but due to a religious observance they could not march on Marathon until the next full moon. So, the historian states, only 11,000 Athenian and Plataean soldiers took the field at Marathon. Miltiades, however, had a plan. Closing rapidly with the Persians would nullify the effects of their archers, who were capable of sending withering showers of arrows on distant enemies. Once the hoplites, or heavy infantry, of the Athenians had come to grips with the enemy, they could deal with the lightly armoured Persian troops with the spear and the short sword. The Persians depended heavily on their archers, while their foot soldiers carried only daggers or short spears and their cavalry swords and axes.

When the battle was joined, it was the speed of the Greek advance and the superiority of their weapons and tactics that won the day at Marathon. Utilizing their phalanx formation, the Greeks made two important modifications. They widened their front to prevent being outflanked, and when they had reached a distance of roughly 100 yards from the Persian line, they broke into a sprint to take the enemy archers by surprise.

The lengthened flanks were necessary, but in turn the Greek centre was weakened. For a time, the invaders appeared on the brink of victory, but when the Persians were put to flight on the flanks, those Greek warriors turned on the Persians who were overextended in the centre.

Herodotus wrote, "Here again they were triumphant, chasing the routed enemy and cutting them down as they ran to the edge of the sea. Then, plunging into the water, they laid hold of the ships, calling for fire."

As they withdrew aboard ship, the Persians still hoped to salvage victory by attacking Athens. If the Persian fleet showed up offshore, Miltiades worried, the city might be compelled to surrender with its army absent. Legend says that Pheidippides, exhausted from his run to Sparta, was then ordered to sprint the 26 miles from Marathon to Athens to deliver the news of the victory. He did so, gasping on arrival, "Rejoice, we conquer!" He then collapsed and died.

By the time Datis and the Persians reached Athens it was too late. The Athenian army had marched swiftly back to the city to stand against the invaders. The Persians had had enough and turned away.

Herodotus wrote that Persian losses at Marathon totalled 6,400 while only 192 Athenians and Plataeans had fallen. While on the march, the Spartans received word of the victory and continued on to view the corpses of the vanquished Persians. The Greeks buried their dead in two great mounds still visible on the battlefield.

The victory at Marathon was quite an achievement for the Athenian democracy. The triumph marked the preservation of Greece and the beginning of an unprecedented advancement of Western culture. Defeat would undoubtedly have altered the course of history.

ABOVE: Greek soldiers crash into the Persian invaders and rout the enemy at the Battle of Marathan, 490 BC. (Public Domain)

LEFT: Fighting at the water's edge, the Greeks repel the invading Persians at the Battle of Marathon. (Public Domain)

THE SECOND PERSIAN WAR

When the news of his great army's defeat at the Battle of Marathon and its subsequent withdrawal reached the court of the Persian King Darius I, his anger spiraled out of control. More determined than ever to conquer Athens and all of Greece, he set about immediately to organize yet another military expedition.

Orders went out to raise an even larger army, and more ships were built to carry the Persian warriors on their mission of conquest. Several years passed as preparations for a renewal of hostilities took place, but Darius I was an old man. He had reigned for 36 years only to experience stinging defeat twice at the hands of the upstart Greeks. He died before he was able to exact revenge, and the responsibility for the honour of the Persian ruling house fell to his son Xerxes. Along with that weight, it would be Xerxes who would decide if and when to attack the Greeks again.

At first, Xerxes appeared to have no real interest in renewing the animosity with the Greeks. After crushing a revolt in Egypt, however, he reconsidered and decided to consult his lieutenants and summoned a council of war to determine the proper course of action against Greece. The king addressed the gathering, "As you saw Darius himself was making preparations for war against these men; but death prevented him from carrying out his purpose. I, therefore on his behalf, and for the benefit of all my subjects, will not rest until I have taken Athens and burnt it to the ground in revenge for the injury which the Athenians without provocation once did to me and my father… If we crush the Athenians and their neighbours in the Peloponnese, we shall so extend the empire of Persia that its boundaries will be God's own sky."

Xerxes apparently gave the assembled noblemen the opportunity to state their

ABOVE: Spartan soldiers throw Persian envoys down a well prior to the second Persian invasion of Greece. (Public Domain)

opinions, and according to Herodotus only the king's uncle, Artabanus, was against pursuing another war of vengeance and conquest against the Greeks.

"I warned your father – Darius my own brother – not to attack the Scythians, those wanderers who live in a cityless land," the old man declared. "But he would not listen to me. Confident in his power to subdue them he invaded their country and before he came home again many fine soldiers who marched with him were dead. But you, my lord, intend to attack a nation greatly superior to the Scythians, a nation with the highest reputation for valour both on land and sea. It is my duty to tell you that you have to fear them. You have said you mean to bridge the Hellespont and march through Europe to Greece. Now suppose –

and it is not impossible – that you were to suffer a reverse by sea or land, or even both. These Greeks are said to be great fighters – and indeed one might well guess as much from the fact that the Athenians alone destroyed the great army we sent to attack them under Datis and Artaphernes. Or, if you will, suppose they were to succeed upon one element only – suppose they fell upon our fleet and defeated it, and then sailed to the Hellespont and destroyed the bridge; then my lord you would indeed be in peril."

The assembly joined the confident Xerxes in laughing at Artabanus, even though he had reminded them of two military disasters that had previously occurred. As the hours passed into night, Xerxes began to ponder his uncle's words and took them to heart, concluding that an attack on the Greeks would be ill advised, even after all the preparations that had occurred.

That night, Xerxes slept fitfully, and in a dream he was supposedly visited by a phantom that prodded him to move ahead with the invasion of Greece. With the dawn, though, he dismissed the dream and gave orders to cancel the entire operation. But the following night the apparition appeared a second time and promised that the kingdom of Persia would be doomed if the military expedition against the Greeks did not proceed. Xerxes was unnerved by this experience and called for Artabanus. He instructed his uncle to wear the king's

Persian Median Elamite Parthian Arian Bactrian Sogdian Choresmian Zarangian Arachosian Sattagydian Gandharan Hindush Saka haumavarga

Saka tigraxauda Babylonian Assyrian Arab Egyptian Armenian Cappadocian Lydian Ionian Overseas Saka Skudrian Ionian with shield-hat Libyan Ethiopian

ABOVE: Soldiers of the Persian Army decorate the tomb of Persian King Xerxes. (Creative Commons A.Davey via Wikipedia)

ABOVE: The huge Persian army under Xerxes crosses the Hellespont, the modern Dardanelles, during the second invasion of Greece. (Public Domain)

clothes, sit on the royal throne for a while, and then sleep in the king's bed that night.

Xerxes concluded that if the spirit appeared to Artabanus, then it was surely sent from the divine. According to legend passed through generations, the spirit did indeed come upon Artabanus in the night, threatening to destroy him for interfering and nearly reaching the point of putting the old man's eyes out with hot irons before Artabanus woke up and ran to Xerxes, approving the invasion. In turn, Xerxes rescinded his earlier order and instructed that the preparations move forward with all haste.

It is worthwhile to consider that this tale was told by Herodotus, a historian renowned

ABOVE: Xerxes watches the lashing of the unruly Hellespont prior to his invasion of Greece. (Public Domain)

for embellishment. While it is probable that some liberties were taken with the facts, it is also true that the Greeks believed that the gods were involved in the daily affairs of mortals. The Greek audience, therefore, responded to the influence of omens and soothsayers with actions that were reflective of their beliefs.

In response to the order from Xerxes, Persian engineers went to work bridging the Hellespont, known in modern times as the Dardanelles. They built two bridges that were 1,400 yards long and supported by 674 ships that acted as pontoons atop which a causeway was laid. The first two bridges were thoroughly destroyed by a tremendous storm, and Xerxes was enraged at the delay. He ordered the engineers who built these spans to be executed and then that the Hellespont itself receive 300 lashes in retribution. A new group of engineers built two replacement bridges while three years of digging opened a canal across an isthmus 1½ miles wide near Mount Athos to bypass the treacherous coastline where the Persian fleet had come to grief in a great storm during the first Persian invasion of Greece.

At long last, a full 10 years after the humiliating defeat at Marathon, the Persian military, apparently invincible in its might, was on the move once more against the Greeks. The army of destiny lumbered forward. Herodotus estimated its strength at an outlandish five million men and stated that they Persian host drank rivers dry as it passed on its way. Estimates of its true strength vary, but many historians agree that the army numbered about 500,000 soldiers and the navy consisted of more than 1,200 triremes.

No doubt, the Athenians and all of Greece were aware that a day of reckoning with the

Persians would come. Near Athens, a rich vein of silver had been discovered in the mines at Larium, and by 482 BC discussions were being held on the highest and best use of that newly discovered wealth. The city's foremost politician at the time was Aristides, and he favoured the strengthening of Athenian land forces. However, his long-time rival, Themistocles, successfully persuaded the gathering that the funds should be used to strengthen the Athenian navy. And so it was decided that a stronger navy would be built. The decision was to be fortuitous.

Xerxes and the Persian army advanced steadily during the summer of 480 BC.

The Capture of the Acropolis by the Persians

ABOVE: A few Athenians resist Persian soldiers assaulting the Acropolis during the burning of Athens. (Public Domain)

ABOVE: This relief depicts a Spartan soldier like those who stood against the Persians.

(Creative Commons Oblomov2 via Wikipedia)

Ceremony of Presenting Earth and Water.

ABOVE: Gifts of earth and water are presented to the Persians as signs of tribute. (Public Domain)

ABOVE: A Greek hoplite falls in battle against the Persian army. (Creative Commons Marco Prins via Wikipedia)

Slight opposition was easily brushed aside as many Greek cities offered earth and water as signs of submission to the invaders. Still, neither Athens nor Sparta intended to bow before the Persian king. The Greek plan relied on holding two key locations to stall the Persian onslaught, the narrow pass at Thermopylae, through which the invaders had to pass en route to Athens, and the cape of Artemisium on the coast of the island of Euboea, where Greek warships might block the movement of the Persian fleet.

In August, while Themistocles moved the Greek fleet to Artemisium, the Spartan King Leonidas advanced to hold the pass at Thermopylae with roughly 7,000 soldiers, including Spartans, Thebans, and other troops from the city states. The fighting at Thermopylae lasted three days, during which Leonidas ordered the bulk of his force to retire while he stood with 300 elite Spartan hoplites to defend the pass against overwhelming odds. In one of the epic stands of military history, the Spartans fought to the last man but bought valuable time, delaying the Persian passage on land while two violent gales wracked their fleet, the second destroying approximately 200 ships that Xerxes had ordered to sail around the island of Euboea to attack the Greeks navy from the rear.

Themistocles had led the Greek fleet to a minor victory in the Gulf of Pagasae. Then,

the naval Battle of Artemisium was fought at the same times as the heroic Spartans sacrificed themselves at Thermopylae. Both fleets had been battered, sustaining heavy casualties. The Athenians could not afford such grievous losses, and when Themistocles received word that Thermopylae had been lost, he executed a tactical withdrawal to the island of Salamis in the Saronic Gulf about 16 kilometres (10 miles) west of Athens.

Once clear of Thermopylae, the Persian army struck rapidly toward Athens, which was virtually abandoned after Themistocles had advised the citizenry to evacuate to Salamis for its best chance of survival. All of northern Greece might later be defenceless against the Persian onslaught, which reached a destructive crescendo when the invaders burned Athens, looted the Acropolis, and then slaughtered any Athenians who had remained in the city.

The wrath of Xerxes was unleashed, but the burning of Athens hardly satisfied his bloodlust. The Persians turned toward

the narrow isthmus that separated the Peloponnese from northern Greece, where the Spartans and other Peloponnesian soldiers had erected a wall to defend their cities and homes. Meanwhile, their naval contingents had joined Themistocles off Salamis. The genius of the Greek naval commander shone through as he deceived Xerxes into weakening his fleet prior to the decisive battle of the Second Persian War. Xerxes fell for a false report that persuaded him to send a squadron of Egyptian ships on a fool's errand. Then, on September 20, 480 BC, the allied Greek fleet decisively defeated the Persians at the Battle of Salamis.

In its wake, Xerxes had little choice but to contemplate a full withdrawal. The Greeks might sail north and destroy the bridges across the Hellespont, cutting supply and communication lines. Weather conditions might turn and destroy what was left of his once proud navy. And most important, should the situation in Greece deteriorate further, the king should be removed from peril and continue to rule his empire from the safety of his capital at Susa.

Xerxes did withdraw much of his land army, leaving 300,000 men in Thessaly under Mardonius, one of the highest-ranking Persian generals. The following spring, Mardonius led his army south and took Athens again. But in the summer of 479 BC, the Spartan and Athenian armies pushed the Persians northward and won a final victory in the Battle of Plataea in September. That same month, the Greek fleet won another victory over the Persians at Mycale, off the Ionian coast.

At last, Greece was free from the threat of Eastern domination. For the next 50 years, Sparta would be the primary Greek military power on land, while Athens was preeminent at sea. The balance of power was maintained for a time, until rivalries and mistrust increased and the next great threat to the future of Greece arose from within.

THE INVASION OF GREECE.

ABOVE: Persian forces advance into Greece, confronting the allied forces of the city states. (No restrictions via Wikipedia)

THE BATTLE OF THERMOPYLAE

Three hundred Spartan soldiers and their leader, Leonidas, are renowned throughout Western history and culture for their heroism and self-sacrifice before the Persian host at the Battle of Thermopylae. Translated literally from the Greek, Thermopylae is known as the "pass of the hot springs."

It was there that the Spartans died to a man defending a space that was said to be barely 50 feet wide at its narrowest point, slowing down the Persian onslaught into Greece and making the invaders pay dearly for possession of pass that led toward Athens. Leonidas ordered the majority of his original force of roughly 7,000 to withdraw to fight another day and stood with his loyal elite hoplites and small contingents from other city states in an epic story of valour.

Although the exact date of the battle remains obscure, around August 18, 480 BC, Xerxes and his mighty army approached the pass at Thermopylae, and the Persian king ordered a series of frontal assaults. The first men forward were Cissians and Medes in the service of the Persians.

ABOVE: Spartan commander Leonidas is depicted at Thermopylae in this romanticized painting by Jacques Louis David. (Public Domain)

ABOVE: Spartans hold fast against the Persian host at the narrow pass of Thermopylae. (Public Domain)

They attacked the Spartans repeatedly but were driven back each time with heavy losses. By late afternoon, Xerxes committed his "Immortals," his own elite combat division whose esprit de corps and daring were the envy of the rest of the Persian army. These experienced troops, under the command of Hydarnes, attacked the Spartans with confidence.

Herodotus, however, told the story of the grim outcome for the Immortals. "But, once again engaged they were no more successful than the Medes had been. All went as before, the two armies fighting in a confined space, the Persians using shorter spears than the Greeks and having no advantage in numbers."

While the narrow space of the pass did aid the defenders, the overwhelming numbers of attacking Persians being forced into a limited zone and unable to outflank the Spartans, Leonidas also utilized deception to his advantage on several occasions. When the opportunity presented itself, perhaps during a lull in the fighting, the Spartans would turn their backs to the Persians and momentarily feign a confused

withdrawal. Excited by the prospect of a complete victory, the Persians would take the bait, charging ahead to finish off the stubborn Spartans. Seconds later, they found themselves in dire straits.

The well-disciplined Spartans would execute a swift about face, turning at the last possible moment to confront the rapidly advancing Persians with spear and sword. In the close quarter melee that followed, the more heavily armed Spartans would slash and stab with

ABOVE: Surrounded by thousands of Persian soldiers, Leonidas and the 300 Spartans fight to the death at Thermopylae. (Public Domain)

The Battle of Thermopylae.

ABOVE: At Thermopylae the Spartans under Leonidas fought to the last man against the Persians. (Public Domain)

reckless abandon, killing scores of astonished Persians that had been lured into the death trap between the rocky cliffsides of the pass.

After hours of fruitless assaults, a frustrated Xerxes decided to withdraw the bulk of his army some distance away from Thermopylae. Perhaps some doubt as to his ability to force passage had crept into his mind, and the sight of his battered and exhausted soldiers was discouraging.

Leonidas and his indomitable Spartans stood their ground for another full day as the sun rose and set over the scene of the slaughter. There was a flicker of hope that the Persians might melt away and leave the defenders in possession of the pass. However, treachery provided the undoing of the heroic Spartans. Ephialtes, a Greek traitor, approached the Persian lines and was taken before King Xerxes. He offered to show the Persians a long route across the nearby mountains that would allow the invaders to attack the Spartans from the rear. Early in the defence of the pass, Leonidas had ordered about 1,000 men from Phocia to guard the extreme rear of the Spartan position. However, when the Phocians saw the mighty host of the Persian army bearing down upon them, they fled the field in panic, opening the back door for the attackers.

With that, the fate of the Spartans was sealed. The Spartans were well aware of what awaited them as news of the oncoming Persian force reached Thermopylae. Their soothsayer spoke openly of the deaths that would come with the dawn. Herodotus wrote, "To the Greeks who were in Thermopylae first the soothsayer Megistias, after looking into the victims which were sacrificed, declared the death which was to come to them at dawn of day; and afterwards deserters brought the report of the Persians having gone round. These signified it to them while it was yet night, and thirdly came the day-watchers, who had run down from the heights when day was already dawning.

"Then the Greeks deliberated, and their opinions were divided; for some urged that they should not desert their post, while others opposed this counsel. After this they departed from their assembly, and some went away and dispersed each to their several cities, while others of them were ready to remain there together with Leonidas."

According to some historians, Leonidas sent more soldiers away from the area either to prevent greater losses or because he noticed that they were wavering in the face of certain death and dismissed them out of contempt.

The Spartan warriors, however, were resolute and disdainful of flight to safety. When one of their number named Dieneces was told that the Persians were bearing down on his position and that the enemy would loose so many arrows at the Spartans

that their flight would darken the sky. His retort remains one of the great quotations of military history. He smiled and said, "This is pleasant news… for if the Persians hide the sun, we shall have our battle in the shade."

When the final desperate battle began, the defenders were assailed from both front and rear. They fought like lions, those who had lost their weapons using their hands, fists and teeth to maintain the struggle. Before they were overwhelmed, the Spartans killed hundreds of Persian soldiers, and among the dead were two of Xerxes' brothers, princes of the realm. Some accounts state that 20,000 Persians were killed at Thermopylae, roughly five times the number of Greek soldiers killed throughout the fight and including the heroic 300.

The Greeks who learned of the awesome courage displayed at Thermopylae were awed by the willingness of the few to give their lives so freely. Herodotus wrote later that he personally committed to memory the names of all 300 Spartan defenders who remained "because they deserved to be remembered." Of course, the 300 have been remembered, revered in both ancient and modern writings, and in recent years on the motion picture screen as well.

Although the Battle of Thermopylae was, after all, a defeat and did not halt the progress of the Persian drive for Athens, it was a watershed moment for the Greeks, who drew inspiration from it. Without doubt, those who opposed the Persians after Thermopylae did so with stouter hearts and a firmer footing in the defence of their homeland.

After the war, the Greeks placed a plaque at Thermopylae to commemorate the bravery of Leonidas and the 300. It read, "Go tell the Spartans, you who read: We took their orders and are dead."

ABOVE: Spartan commander Leonidas sends a message from embattled Thermopylae while holding out against the Persians. (Public Domain)

ABOVE: This relief is believed to depict the famed Immortals of the Persian army, decimated at Thermopylae by the Spartans. (Public Domain)

ABOVE: The Persian fleet is shattered at the Battle of Salamis in this painting by Wilhelm von Kaulbach. (Public Domain)

THE BATTLE OF SALAMIS

The decisive battle that put paid the threat of the Persian military and the vengeful King Xerxes did not take place on land but at sea. The Athenian politician Themistocles had argued in favour of building a strong naval contingent and predicted that the outcome of a sea fight would spell victory or defeat in the second Greek war with Persia.

Themistocles and his long-time rival, Aristeides, had debated the best use of the wealth that Athens reaped from the mining of a large vein of silver at Laurium two years before the decisive Battle of Salamis. Aristeides, the first citizen of Athens, had been a forceful proponent of augmenting the Athenian land forces, but Themistocles won the day. Soon enough, the construction of a mighty fleet was begun in Athens, and when it was put to the test, the Athenian navy triumphed. To his credit, Aristeides later became a prominent military commander and gave his full support to Themistocles when the fighting began at Salamis.

The second Persian invasion of Greece had been via both land and sea. The Persian army, once past the tenacious Spartan defenders of the pass at Thermopylae, marched toward Athens. Themistocles had advised the evacuation of the city, and most of the citizenry had complied. The Persians plundered and burned Athens, but subsequently their way north was blocked by

BELOW: The Greek trireme was a versatile ship of war and commerce. (Public Domain)

the Spartans and other Greek forces at the narrow isthmus that led to their cities and homes in the region. And then there was the Athenian fleet and its allies to deal with as well.

Military analysts have observed that Xerxes allowed his eagerness to fight a decisive battle at sea get the better of his judgment. According to Herodotus, Queen Artemisia of Halicarnassus had advised against a headlong rush to battle at sea. "If you do not hurry to fight at sea, but keep your ships here and stay near land, or even advance into the Peloponnese, then, my lord, you will easily accomplish what you had in mind on coming here. The Hellenes are not able to hold out against you for a long time,

but you will scatter them, and they will each flee to their own cities," she offered. But Xerxes was determined.

The weapon of decision at sea in those ancient days was the trireme, a multi-purpose vessel that was common among the fleets of the Mediterranean world from the 7th century BC to the 4th century BC. The trireme dominated naval battles of the period and also carried cargo as a merchant vessel. The trireme derived its name from the three rows of 30 oars on both the starboard and port sides of the ship. A total of 180 oarsmen powered the vessels, which were typically about 37 metres long with a shallow draft of about a metre and a height above the waterline

ABOVE: Greek triremes fall upon the confused Persian enemy, ramming their vessels during the Battle of Salamis. (Public Domain)

ABOVE: The Persian admiral Ariabignes, brother of Xerxes, dies in battle at Salamis. (Public Domain)

power, the Athenian fleet was composed of at least 200 triremes. These were to be employed skilfully by Themistocles at Salamis.

Before the Battle of Salamis was joined, Themistocles successfully weakened his opponent's strength. He concocted a false tale and ordered one of his slaves to deliver a message to Xerxes. Herodotus explained that the slave, named Sicinnus, told the Persians, "I am the bearer of a secret communication from the Athenian commander, who is a well-wisher to your king and hopes for a Persian victory. He has told me to report to you that the Greeks have no confidence in themselves and are planning to save their skins by a hasty withdrawal. Only prevent them from slipping through your fingers and you have at this moment an opportunity for unparalleled success. They are at daggers drawn with each other, and will offer no opposition – on the contrary, you will see the pro-Persians amongst them fighting the rest."

Xerxes was astonished but gratefully accepted the slave's misinformation as fact. He then weakened his force by sending a squadron of Egyptian vessels to seal off a possible Athenian escape route; therefore, these triremes would not be available during the decisive battle. Xerxes ordered more triremes to cover the channel near Cape Cynosura, and when these movements were completed, he intended to order his fleet forward to annihilate the Greeks in the narrow waters off Salamis. He took his seat on a golden throne high above the sea after ordering the main body of the Persian armada, roughly 400 triremes, forward on the morning of September 20, 480 BC, and settled back to watch the battle unfold.

Themistocles arrayed the Greek fleet with his Athenians on the left of his defensive line, the experienced Corinthians covering the Bay of Eleusis in the north, and the Peloponnesian ships on the right with the triremes from the city states of Megara and Aegina close by in Ambelaki Bay. He purposely concealed the majority of the 300 triremes under his command around St. George's Island, out of sight of the approaching Persians. Themistocles hoped to draw the Persians into

ABOVE: Artemisia, queen of Halicarnassus, shoots arrows at the Greeks before fleeing from Salamis. (Public Domain)

the narrow confines around Salamis and well into shallow water that would restrict their movement. He ordered the 50 Corinthian triremes to hoist their square sails and feign a retreat, allowing the Persians to observe their apparently panicked manoeuvre.

Once the Persians were committed to the shallows and perhaps in pursuit of the Corinthians, the Greeks would emerge in an orderly line and surround them. Such a movement would neutralize the Persian numerical advantage. The greater number of ships might actually hinder their ability to manoeuvre in the narrow confines and shallow waters. As the battle unfolded, the Persians responded to the ruse, just as Themistocles had hoped. They sailed into their own undoing.

Herodotus reported that the Greek oarsmen and sailors began to sing a hymn to the god Apollo as they fell upon the exposed left flank of the Persian vanguard. When the commanders of the Persian ships realized that they were being trapped and surrounded, they ordered their oarsmen to backwater. However, this action only magnified their predicament, creating tremendous confusion and a crush of ship against ship with some moving forward and others moving to the rear. The Persian

of approximately two metres, presenting a low profile. A pair of rudders at the stern were used for steering, and a square sail was hoisted on the mainmast amidships while the foremast was rigged with sail as well.

The trireme was constructed of light wood and highly mobile. It is believed that its weight could be supported and carried a short distance, perhaps from the water onto the shore, by a complement of 140 men. The ship could sail right onto a beach for the discharge of cargo or soldiers. Before going into battle, the trireme's masts were taken down and stored, and each vessel was equipped at the bow with a heavy bronze ram, its impact intended to shatter the hull of an opposing warship. At the height of its

ABOVE: After the victory at Salamis, Themistocles comes ashore in triumph. (Public Domain)

ABOVE: Themistocles presides over a sacrifice to the gods before going into battle at Salamis. (Public Domain)

ABOVE: At Salamis Greek triremes sail into battle against the larger Persian fleet. (Public Domain)

the Phoenicians scurried up the cliffside to the throne of Xerxes and swore that the Ionian sailors fighting alongside them were the cause of the defeat. Xerxes had watched the Ionians during the one-sided debacle and determined that they had fought bravely. He ordered the cowardly Phoenicians beheaded for lying about their allies.

Estimates of the Persian losses at Salamis run as high as 200 triremes, while Greek losses are believed to have been around 40 warships. In the wake of the disaster, Xerxes held a council of war to determine his next move. Even as the council convened, Persian men were being killed by the score on both land and sea.

Herodotus wrote that Mardonius, a trusted Persian general, minimized the magnitude of the defeat at Salamis and addressed Xerxes. "Sire," he pleaded, "be not grieved nor greatly distressed because of what has befallen us. It is not on things of wood that the issue hangs for us, but on men and horses...If then you so desire, let us straightway attack the Peloponnese, or if it pleases you to wait, that also we can do...It is best then that you should do as I have said, but if you have resolved to lead your army away, even then I have another plan. Do not, O king, make the Persians the laughing-stock of the Greeks, for if you have suffered harm, it is by no fault of the Persians...."

In the end, Xerxes withdrew most of his forces from Greece and left Mardonius with an army of 300,000 to continue the fight. Although he met with initial success and occupied Athens for a second time, Mardonius ultimately was defeated at Plataea in the final battle of the Persian Wars.

ABOVE: His vision of a strong Athenian navy vindicated, Themistocles was the victor over the Persians at Salamis. (Public Domain)

ships coming behind the lead element simply had nowhere to go.

The famed playwright Aeschylus, father of Greek tragedy, fought at Salamis and at the decisive Battle of Marathon a decade earlier. His remembrance of the Persian entrapment at sea was likened to the mass netting and killing of fish on the shores of the Mediterranean Sea. "At first the torrent of the Persians' fleet bore up, but then the press of shipping hemmed them in the narrows; none could help another."

Writing from the Persian point of view, Aeschylus continued, "The hulls of our vessels rolled over and the sea was hidden from our sight, choked with wrecks and slaughtered men. The shores and reefs were strewn with corpses. In wild disorder every ship remaining in our fleet turned tail and fled. But the Greeks pursued us, and with oars or broken fragments of wreckage struck the survivors' heads as though they were tunneys and a haul of fish. Shrieks and groans rang across the water until nightfall hid us from them."

The Greeks had kept out of the tangle of Persian triremes and struck the most

vulnerable virtually at will. The Persian triremes were larger and sat higher in the water than their Greek counterparts, much more suited for naval warfare in open spaces. Further, their decks were packed with as many as 30 marine infantry and archers. In contrast, the sleek Greek triremes carried only 14 fighting men aboard. In the close quarter Battle of Salamis, the Persian warships made easy targets for the heavy bronze rams installed on the Greek triremes.

Queen Artemisia was in the thick of the fight, leading her contingent of triremes against the Greek alliance. As Xerxes looked on, he saw the queen's warship attack and ram another Persian vessel in the confusion as she attempted to escape the trap. Thinking Artemisia had vanquished an Athenian ship and watching his other captains performing so poorly, Xerxes wailed, "My men have become women, and my women men."

A number of Phoenician sailors were present with the Persian fleet, and several of their triremes were run aground intentionally as they broke under the relentless pressure of the Greeks. A few of

THE BATTLE OF PLATAEA

The devastating defeat at the naval Battle of Salamis in 480 BC left the Persian King Xerxes on the horns of a dilemma – stay and fight with all his military might or return to his capital at Susa with the bulk of his army while leaving adequate forces to continue the subjugation of the Greek city states on land and sea.

Xerxes chose the latter course, leaving his capable lieutenant Mardonius in command of 300,000 archers, infantry, and cavalry, including about 50,000 Greek troops from city states such as Thebes that had sworn loyalty to the Persians. Surely, Xerxes believed, this would be sufficient to defeat the allied Greek armies, led by Sparta and Athens. During the Second Persian War, Xerxes had increased his dominion over much of Greece; however, he had yet to conquer the Peloponnese, and the Persian forces outnumbered the Greeks roughly three to one.

In the summer of 479 BC, nearly a year after Salamis, the Greeks marshalled their forces and marched out of the Peloponnese with Pausanias in command to confront the invaders. Mardonius, however, initially declined to offer battle, marching his forces into Boetia in central Greece and establishing a base at Plataea. He hoped to induce the Greeks to attack his fortified position across open ground, favourable for his swift cavalry to envelop an advancing force and providing a clear field of fire for his archers.

This time, however, the Greeks declined to fight on Persian terms. The two sides watched one another for 11 days. Skirmishing occurred, but the Greeks repelled a strong force of Persian cavalry, killing its commander, Masistius. A few days later, Mardonius sent his cavalry around the Greek flank to interdict their supply lines. The Persian horsemen fell upon a column guarded by poorly armed Greek soldiers and slaughtered them, putting the supplies to the torch. Persian archers watched the banks of a nearby river, and the Greeks' thirst grew each

ABOVE: In close quarter combat at Plataea, Greek hoplites repel an attack by the Persians. (Public Domain)

ABOVE: The Persian commander Masistius is killed in action during the decisive Battle of Plataea. (Public Domain)

ABOVE: Aristeides tells ambassadors from the Persian general Mardonius that Greece will never submit to the rule of Xerxes. (Public Domain)

day. The Persian horsemen further harassed the Greeks when they approached their main source of water, a local spring.

Pausanias realized his water shortage was critical and manoeuvred to secure it under cover of darkness. In the resulting confusion, the entire left flank of the Greek army was left unsupported. The Persians seized the opportunity to attack these exposed troops and appeared to gain the upper hand. At the critical moment, however, the Greek right flank turned to assist their hard-pressed comrades. The Persians had committed fully to the fight, their centre coming up behind their vanguard, vulnerable to counterattack. The heavily armed and armoured Greek hoplites routed the lighter equipped Persians, slashing through their wicker shields with sword and spear and putting them to flight.

Mardonius was killed in the fighting as his command was forced back into its reinforced positions at Plataea. The Greek centre joined the fight but took heavy casualties in a poorly led advance, but Pausanias reorganized and led his army in storming the Persian encampment. The Greeks killed scores of Persians, destroying the fighting capability of the invaders. Soon, the Greeks turned toward Thebes, exacting vengeance by looting and burning the traitorous city.

As Persian designs on conquest in Greece crumbled, the Greek navy scored a resounding victory over the Persian fleet at Mycale off the Ionian coast. The power of Persian arms was broken, and Xerxes never invaded Greece again. The string of Greek military victories from Salamis to Plataea and Mycale had ensured the future of Western culture, which thrived in the years to come.

ANCIENT GREEK SOCIETY

ABOVE: Two ancient Greek women weave a tapestry in this painting by artist Josephine Houssaye. (Public Domain)

Across the centuries, the ancient Greek city states experimented with various forms of government, including the years of the tyrants, the investiture of kings, and the noble experiments in democracy which began in Athens and spread across Greece and then even into the cities of the Persian Empire.

Greek society became more cosmopolitan through the centuries as territories were explored and conquered, colonies were established, and foreign cultures and individuals were extant or assimilated into the widening world view of the people. Always, however, Greek society was tied to the land. Farming was the cornerstone of Greek economic stability and the source of initial prosperity, and later the wealth and affluence of an emergent ruling class.

The ancient Greek social structure was clearly defined in a hierarchy that began with the male citizenry, men who occupied three broad categories, the affluent or aristocratic, the artisans and traders, and the farmers. Male citizens were the most influential of Greek society. In most cases they were the owners of property, cast votes in elections, and were qualified to hold public office.

The aristocratic class possessed most of the wealth, generally held the highest public offices, and consolidated its power within a relative few elite families. The aristoi, as they were called, were financially capable of furnishing their own armour, weapons, equipment, and horses in the event of a military campaign.

The merchant or business class, which included some landowners, farmers, and producers and sellers of finished goods, were newly well to do, achieving some measure of financial success through the conduct of trade and commerce. Although they were challenged in regard to upward social mobility, these individuals and families constituted an emerging middle class whose economic influence and numbers increased over time and ultimately could not be ignored. The polarity of the "class struggle" between the merchant and the aristoi classes became increasingly relevant in ancient Greek society with the passage of time.

While the aristoi derived their wealth from land ownership and agricultural production, they also benefited from close proximity to the protection of city walls. In the event of conflict, they found shelter more quickly than the poorer landowners, known as the perioikoi. These farmers occupied land further from the city walls, perhaps of inferior quality, and in some cases yielding crops of little more than subsistence levels. The perioikoi were often located far enough from larger population centres that they gathered in smaller villages for protection and social interaction. This class was prone to significant growth across generations as populations expanded and wealth was divided among family members.

Other classes included the labourers, or helots as they were known in Sparta, and the slave population. The helots were workers or serfs who held a status somewhere between the slave and the citizen. They were not bought and sold as property and often made deals with their employers to provide a share of their farm production in exchange for the privilege of cultivating a particular plot. In a sense

ABOVE: A flute player entertains bakers kneading bread in this clay figurine. (Creative Commons Marie-Lan Nguyen via Wikipedia)

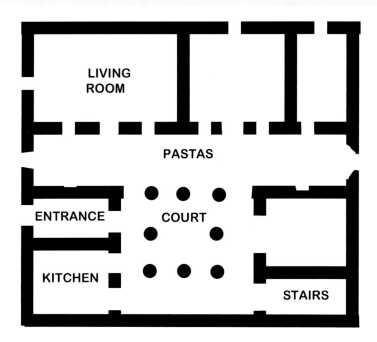

MAISON DE LA COLLINE DELOS

ABOVE: This floorplan depicts an ancient Greek house of the 2nd century BC. (Public Domain)

Some surviving records from the region of Thessaly indicate that women did own property in rare instances there.

Marriages were arranged by the father of a young woman, and he accepted a dowry from the chosen husband. Typically, girls married at the tender age of 13 or 14, and marriages could be annulled under only three circumstances, rejection by the husband with return of the dowry, the father of the bride requiring the return of his daughter to offer her to another man with a more valuable dowry, or the bride deserting the home for some specific reason. The third situation rarely occurred due to the social stigma it carried.

The lot of Spartan women stood as a notable exception to that of most city states. Sparta was a militaristic society, and the men were routinely serving in the army, perhaps away on a campaign. The women,

ABOVE: A theatre performance is shown in progress in this artwork from a decorative vase. (Public Domain)

that aspect of their existence was similar to a 19th century sharecropper in rural America.

The helots also farmed land owned by the state. They were often subject to brutal treatment by their Spartan overlords, and during wartime they were regularly obliged to serve in the military. Opportunities to improve their social status was virtually non-existent. However, if they rendered valuable military service, some helots actually were able to rise to an elevated class that was still inferior to full citizenry.

Slaves were acquired through warfare, purchase from merchants, or even abduction. Their lot in life was to serve their masters, and they were an integral and accepted part of Greek society. The slaves who worked in households performing domestic tasks fared better than those who laboured in fields or mines, and at any given time the slave population of Athens was estimated at 30 percent of the total. Slaves were property, bought and sold, subject to the justice or mercy of their masters, and sometimes became skilled artisans working in gold, silver, and leather. Others worked as clerks, rowers, commercial traders, and entertainers.

In some documented cases, slaves earned trusted positions in their masters' business enterprises and were treated as close associates. However, in most situations the air of apprehension, fear, resentment and mistrust was as common between slave and master in ancient Greece as anywhere else at any time in history.

Women in ancient Greece were seen as societally inferior to the male citizenry. In many cases, they were not allowed to vote or own property. They were not involved in the political discourse or in the affairs of

state. Their purpose was to run the home, rear children, engaging in activities such as meal preparation and domestic chores. Women did participate in religious rituals, but for the most part they were solely responsible for the smooth operation of the household. Women of wealthier families might depend more on slave labour, while poorer women were required to work on their own, often helping with farm chores.

PAUSANIAS OFFERING SACRIFICE TO THE GODS BEFORE HIS GREAT BATTLE.

ABOVE: Ancient Greeks perform a ritual sacrifice to the gods. (Public Domain)

ABOVE: A funerary banquet is depicted in this detailed stone relief of the 4th century BC.
(Creative Commons George E. Koronaios via Wikipedia)

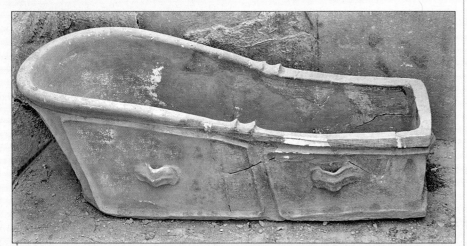

ABOVE: This ancient soaking tub dates to the period of Knossos in the island of Crete.
(Creative Commons Le Plombier du désert via Wikipedia)

as viable individuals until they were five days old, and when they were accepted a ceremony was held to complete the process of incorporating the child into the family.

The practice of pederasty, an older male entering into a sexual relationship with a younger boy, was a common practice. Pederasty also involved a mentoring process as the youth gained insight into the older participant's experience in life.

The homes of most ancient Greeks were simply constructed of bricks formed from mud and then covered in plaster. Pottery tile formed the roof, and the homes of the poor were limited typically to three or fewer rooms. Wealthy families lived in larger houses often decorated with gardens and perhaps including a second level. Common areas such as a dining room and living room were adjacent to the kitchen on the first floor, while bedrooms were upstairs along with a separate room where women ate their meals excluded from the company of men. The wealthier the homeowner, the finer the furnishings.

Public toilets consisted of large rooms with long bench seats connected to efficient drainage networks, while homes of the middle class and the wealthy were sometimes constructed with toilet facilities that drained into a sewer system that ran beneath the city streets. Small stones were used for personal hygiene.

The Greeks cleaned and groomed themselves using olive oil, rubbing themselves thoroughly, and then using a tool called a strigil to scrape the oil from their bodies. A large pottery basin called a louterion was used to hold the oil and then the detritus.

The ancient Greeks worshipped a pantheon of gods and goddesses. They participated in annual religious festivals and observances, offering sacrifices to the deities. They assigned human attributes to their gods and believed that they interacted with humans regularly. The ancient Greek concept of an afterlife is described thoroughly in the Odyssey of Homer. Greeks believed that the spirit of the departed exited the body immediately as a small puff or breath or wind. Proper burial ritual was required and usually performed by women

therefore, were left to maintain the social fabric of Sparta. For these reasons primarily, Spartan women routinely ran the farms and households of the city state. They directed the work of slaves and supervised domestic operations. In Sparta, women could legally own property and inherit estates of deceased relatives. They were often more highly educated than the women of other Greek city states, and many Spartan women amassed substantial wealth and wielded strong influence in the halls of government. Of course, such circumstances sometimes drew criticism from leaders in other city states where women were more subservient.

Spartan mothers understood that raising children, particularly boys who would one day serve in the Spartan army, was their highest duty. Spartan women delegated to their slaves the tasks that women of other city states routinely accepted as their own responsibility – for the Spartan woman certain jobs were simply beneath their dignity. Spartan mothers nevertheless knew their roles well and accepted the primacy of the state and its commitment to military strength. A Spartan mother once told her son as he prepared to go to war that she expected his return "either with your shield

or on it!" Only a coward would drop his shield and flee. One who bravely sacrificed his life for Sparta would have his body brought home with the shield as his catafalque.

In ancient Greece, children of the wealthy were generally well educated, learning to read, write, and perform basic mathematics before their studies turned to literature, philosophy, poetry and music. Spartan boys underwent indoctrination into the military tradition, rigorous physical training, and fighting techniques, while young men of Athens were required to serve a portion of their lives, usually from age 18-20, in some civil capacity or in the military. Basic education began at home, and girls were taught early by their mothers. In addition to learning the skills necessary to run the household, many girls were taught to read and write as well. The Greeks used an alphabet of 24 letters, and children learned to write on clay or wax tablets that could be reused as the surface was wiped smooth from lesson to lesson.

Families were legally permitted to abandon newborn babies, leaving them to die or to be adopted by strangers, if they were found to be physically or mentally deficient. Children were not usually regarded

ABOVE: In this ancient decoration, a student engages in a writing lesson. (Creative Commons via Wikipedia)

GREEK.   11.   ANCIENT TIMES.

1. Philosopher. 2. Citizen. 3. Priest of Ceres. 4. 6. Priests of Bacchus. 5. Female Bacchanant. 7. Priestess. 8-13. Warriors.

ABOVE: Examples of ancient Greek civilian and military dress include simple tunics for men and women. (Public Domain)

ABOVE: Under the watchful eye of his teacher, a student works diligently on his lesson. (Public Domain)

folded and pinned together with a tie at the waist or a long tunic called a chiton along with a himation. Jewellery and long hair were common. Typically, women did not cut their hair unless they were in mourning.

Ancient Greek peoples engaged in leisure activities as time permitted. Great amphitheatres were constructed for audiences to attend performances of comedy and tragedy as drama became a form of art. These theatres could regularly seat several thousand people and were carved in stone into hillsides or naturally bowl-shaped areas, where the acoustics were remarkably good. Listening to music was another favourite pastime.

The Olympic games and other athletic competitions were held, drawing large numbers of spectators. The ancient Greeks also enjoyed storytelling, hunting, and great feasts and banquets. Contests were held in the larger cities as poets, playwrights, and authors gathered to read their works before judges who presented prizes to the winners.

in three parts, the laying out of the body, the funeral procession, and the interment of the body or the cremated ashes.

The archaeological record reveals many lavish monuments erected in remembrance of the dead, particularly those who had come from some financial means in life. The Greeks believed that actual immortality was strongly influenced by the living in

ABOVE: A woman enjoys a swing during a break from her household responsibilities in this decorative image. (Creative Commons Marie-Lan Nguyen via Wikipedia)

remembering the departed. Sculpture and decoration on ancient vases called lekythoi indicate that Greek women regularly visited the resting places of the dead and brought with them offerings of food and drink. In many cases the sculpture, statuary, and memorial columns in the cemeteries were painted in bright colours.

The ancient Greek diet consisted mainly of goat cheese and bread made from barley or wheat, fish, and vegetables. Red meat was seldom consumed, but olives and onions were plentiful along with a variety of fruits. Sometimes eggs were eaten. Small game such as rabbits or birds were often roasted, and wine diluted with water was the common drink. Poorer people drank water sometimes sweetened with a drizzle of honey.

Greek men dressed in a simple wool tunic with a belt or tie at the waist, and in colder weather a cloak called a himation was worn over the left shoulder and tucked under the right. Expensive cotton or silk fabrics were typically reserved for the wealthy, while hats with broad brims were common to shield the wearer in harsh sunlight. Women wore a rectangular cloth called a peplos, which was

ABOVE: An ancient Greek athlete performs acrobatics in a drawing on a vase. (Creative Commons Jastrow via Wikipedia)

GREEK MYTHOLOGY

Mankind has endeavoured to explain its own existence since the beginning of time. The wonders and mysteries of the human experience, the phenomena of earth and heavens, and the basis of life in the physical and metaphysical realms have given rise to myth and legend. Stories of the origins of life, interactions with supernatural beings, began in the oral tradition and were passed down through generations. Repeated and embellished they became a part of religion and tradition, later set down in the written record.

The origin of Greek mythology is mysterious in itself. The ancient Greek tradition that developed into a pantheon of gods and demigods and other fabled creatures is believed to have its origins in the Bronze Age more than 3,000 years ago. It is possible that the stories of gods and heroes passed down through the centuries bear some influence from the kingdoms of the Near East and other ancient civilizations that flourished in the Mediterranean before and during the earliest of Greek religious and mystical stirrings.

The famed Greek historian Herodotus asserted that the Greek pantheon was appropriated or borrowed from the Egyptian culture, and such a conclusion is logical considering the similarities in some of their gods and the parallels of their stories. As the Christian church proliferated, scholars sometimes attributed the Greek gods to characters and themes that originated in Biblical texts from the Jewish tradition. Such might include the Biblical Samson, a character of great physical strength like the Greek Heracles, known to later Romans as Hercules. In addition to their physical attributes, both engage in mortal combat with a lion, and both are betrayed by women.

Other academic theories for the origin of Greek mythology abound. An allegorical interpretation suggests that all mythological characters are symbolic, while the historical theory states that the gods were actually human beings whose exploits were embellished over the years until they took on supernatural attributes. The physical theory offers that natural elements such as wind, rain, and fire were considered phenomena that were supernatural and that the gods were personifications of them. Without doubt, other Indo-European civilizations contributed to the development of the pantheon of Greek gods.

Unlike many other major religions such as Christianity and Islam, whose foundations and rationale are found in the text of a single book, numerous ancient writings

ABOVE: This bust is believed to depict the ancient Greek poet Hesiod. (Public Domain)

ABOVE: Shown in this mosaic, Mnemosyne was the Titan goddess of time, memory and remembrance. (Creative Commons Carolina Lena Becker via Wikipedia)

contributed to the early and in turn the modern understanding of Greek mythology, including its major figures and its principles. Homer goes into detail on the origin and development of the gods in the epic poems of the Iliad and the Odyssey. Thirty-three Homeric Hymns, written anonymously, describe the different gods and pay tribute to them. Hesiod, a contemporary of Homer, is known for numerous works, particularly the Theogony, regarding the foundation of the world, the origins of the gods, and the struggles that ensued. These two towering literary figures are believed to have established the basic tenets and worship customs of Greek religion.

ABOVE: Uranus is shown in happy times surrounded by the dancing stars. (Public Domain)

ABOVE: Gaia and an attendant are shown among the heavens in this painting in the Academy of Fine Arts in Vienna. (Public Domain)

ABOVE: Cronus attacks Uranus in this fanciful artist's rendering of the fabled episode. (Public Domain)

Hesiod was an authority on economics, agriculture, astronomy, and the concept of time, but he is probably best remembered for his writing in the Theogony that deals with the birth of the gods. His account appears to combine the creation myths of the Babylonian and Mycenaean cultures along with some local traditions to produce a blended version of the story. While it is reasonable to view Hesiod's account as foundational to Greek mythology, it is also fair to describe the work as an assessment of the Greek perspective on the known world, serving to validate certain points of view, such as the right of a monarch to govern along with other social standards and themes. Hesiod includes the story of creation, the struggle for supremacy, and the genealogy of the gods, and his work was probably intended for performance as a hymn associated with worship rituals or poetic competitions.

The archetypal event of creation, bringing forth something out of nothing, provides the opening theme of the Theogony. Only darkness and void are apparent as Chaos, or Chasm, reigns. No explanation is given for the rise of the earliest gods from the realm of nothingness, but some interpretations mention the formation of an egg within the darkness of Chaos, and from this the first gods are said to have emerged. Hesiod sees Chaos as a physical place as well as the first of the supernatural beings, gloomy, dark and distant, but to other ancient writers Chaos was only air or atmosphere.

In the 5th century BC, the philosopher Xenophanes described Chaos as the foundation of reality. He wrote, "The upper

ABOVE: The Cyclopes, monster children of Gaia and Uranus, work at their fiery forge. (Public Domain)

limit of the earth borders on air, near our feet. The lower limit reaches down to the apeiron. The sources and limits of the earth, the sea, the sky… and all things are located in a great windy gap, which seems to be infinite, and is a later specification of Chaos."

The word "apeiron" translates into English as "the unlimited." The Greeks were well acquainted with the concept of infinity, and they believed that their existence was a byproduct of basic unity, apeiron, the permanent basis of all things.

Mother Earth, or Gaia, was the first child of Chaos, followed by Tartarus, the underworld or great abyss, Erebus, the darkness that surrounds the underworld, Nyx,

ABOVE: In this 17th century painting, Cronus devours one of his children. (Public Domain)

transform themselves into different life forms such as elements of nature. According to Hesiod, other offspring of Gaia and Uranus were the three Cyclops, born with one large eye in the centre of their foreheads, and three frightening monsters, the Hecatonchieres, with 50 heads and 100 arms each. These children would later prove to be the undoing of their father as they were forced to take sides when the relationship between their parents devolved from one of balanced love and hate to sheer animosity.

Nyx and Erberus also entered into a union and produced Ether, the heavenly light, and Day, the earthly light. Other offspring of Nyx included Fate, Doom, Sleep, Death, Dreams, Nemesis, Deception, Labour, Misery, and many other beings that personified physical pain, emotion and inevitable human experiences.

The ancient Greeks contemplated the universe and concluded that Uranus was its ruler while the cosmos existed as a brass dome with stars sprinkled liberally across its vastness. Uranus, however, was not well suited for the role of either husband or father. As Gaia was painfully giving birth to the Hecatonchieres, Uranus was repulsed by the sight of the monsters and pushed each of them back into their mother's womb, where they were imprisoned. Gaia enlisted the help of her children, the Titans and the Cyclopes, in seeking revenge against Uranus for the excruciating experience.

ABOVE: Rhea watches unable to intervene as Cronus eats one of his children alive. (Public Domain)

the darkness that covers the earth, and Eros, the goddess of love or physical attraction. Hesiod describes Tartarus as a deep abyss, so deep that an anvil of bronze falling from heaven would reach earth in nine days, and another nine days would be required for the anvil to fall from earth to Tartarus.

Nyx is shown in mythology as a winged charioteer or goddess with a misty shroud of darkness hanging about her head. She was the physical embodiment of the night. Erebus kept close company with Nyx in the role of primordial god of darkness. As night fell on the earth, Nyx was said to have carried Erebus across the sky, filling all spaces with the darkness she carried. It followed that the daughters of light belonging to Erebus would come forward each morning and scatter the darkness.

Often depicted as a child of Aphrodite, the later goddess of love, Eros was nevertheless a primordial god. He was mischievous and sometimes seen as a young man bearing gifts that one lover might give to another, and he was the catalyst for love among mortals and gods as well.

Gaia later gave birth to Uranus, the sky, and to Pontus, the sea. Gaia then became both mother and wife to Uranus. From their union, she gave birth to the 12 Titans, a new generation of beings with god-like characteristics, some exhibiting superhuman strength and others with the ability to

ABOVE: The Giants are defeated in this painting by 17th century artist Jacob Jordaens. (Public Domain)

ABOVE: Rhea appears pensive in this 19th century painting by Raffaello Sorbi. (Public Domain)

ABOVE: The war between the gods and the Titans rages in this colourful image from the early 17th century. (Public Domain)

The children of Uranus feared their father. Only Cronus, the last one of the 12 Titans to be born, could muster the will to oppose Uranus. On a particular evening as Uranus approached Gaia's bed, Cronus was hiding out of sight. He took a sickle of flint that his mother had made and given to him, striking Uranus and castrating his father, who began writhing in agony. The Theogony departs from other versions of the story in asserting that Cronus acted on his own initiative; these other accounts assert that four of his brother Titans held Uranus in place while Cronus slashed their father.

The blood that dripped from Uranus's wound formed the Ash Tree Nymphs, or Meliae, and the Honey Nymphs, who were probably among these new beings, played an important part some time later as the infant Zeus was raised on the island of Crete. The blood of Uranus also produced the Giants, who would do battle with the gods of Mount Olympus in the future. The Giants possessed immense physical strength but were not great in stature. Demi-gods of the underworld also sprang from the blood of Uranus. These included the Furies, or Erinyes, each of whom portrayed base qualities of the human spirit, such as Allecto, unceasing in anger, Megaera, jealousy, and Tisiphone, avenger of murder, who came to earth to apprehend criminals and exact judgment upon them for their wicked ways.

In a rage of anger, Cronus took up his father's severed testicles and hurled them far into the sea. Out of a frothy swirl, the beautiful figure of Aphrodite rose to the surface. She glided along the waters and stepped onto the Mediterranean island of Cyprus, which then became sacred to those who worshipped the goddess of love.

Interestingly, the Theogony is silent as to the ultimate fate of the wounded Uranus.

Before his death or his complete withdrawal from the affairs of gods and men, he pronounced a chilling prophecy that the Titans would be punished harshly for plotting against and then mutilating their own father.

Some interpretations of the rise of Cronus indicate that he was motivated not only by the desire to avenge his mother's suffering but also because he was envious of Uranus and overcome by his own desire for absolute power. When Cronus, ironically also known as the god of fertility, injured his father, he disregarded his mother's wishes that the Hecatonchieres and the Cyclopes should be free. Rather, he imprisoned them. Variations on the Theogony state that Gaia also predicted that one day Cronus would be overthrown by his own children.

According to the Theogony, Cronus banished the Hecatonchieres, who hated him with gusto, and the Cyclopes, to Tartarus. Cronus proved himself the strongest of the 12 Titans, which included five brothers and six sisters. He was also believed to be the god of time, particularly when the passage of time was a destructive or detrimental influence.

Among the other Titans, Oceanus, the eldest, was the god of the seas and of the River Okeanos, which was believed to be the source of all fresh water, rain clouds, rivers and streams on earth. Oceanus, usually depicted in Greek mythology with the horns of a bull and the tail of a fish, was also the god of the heavenly bodies and planets that rose and set every day in and out of his

ABOVE: This engraving shows the Titans in chains as they are imprisoned in Tartarus. (Public Domain)

ABOVE: Lightning bolts in hand, Zeus is shown at the reins of his celestial chariot. (Public Domain)

ABOVE: This artist's conception of the Hecatonchieres is quite imposing. (Creative Commons Vampire285 via Wikipedia)

played an important role in the genealogy of the gods through his offspring.

Hyperion, god of the sun, was the father of Helios, the sun, Selene, the moon, and Eos, the dawn. His name translated as "he who goes above," and he was husband to his sister, Theia, the lady of the blue sky. Some creation variations name Hyperion as one of four brothers who served as pillars to separate the four corners of earth and heaven. Hyperion was the easternmost pillar, some said, because the sun rises in the east. He was responsible for the cycle of the days and months that corresponded to the movements of the constellations and the changing of the seasons. Theia, the goddess of sight and heavenly light, was the mother of Helios, Selene, and Eos and was believed to have given gold and silver their lustrous sheen.

The southernmost pillar separating earth and sky was held by Crius, represented by the ram and the constellation Aries, rising in the south and signalling the beginning of the ancient Greek new year. With his partner Eurybia, who was an offspring of the seas, Crius fathered Astraios, the god of the stars.

The Titan Iapetus held the pillar of the west. Potentially a reference to the mortality of human beings, his name translates from the Greek as "the piercer," possibly indicating that he held a spear. He was also known as the god of craftsmanship, while his sons were given significant roles in the shaping of the human condition. Menoetius was arrogant and violent, two characteristics of human behaviour that are generally abhorred. Prometheus, who brought fire to the human race, was known as a schemer

ABOVE: The ancient Greeks worshipped Hera as queen of the gods and wife of Zeus. (Public Domain)

waters. Along with his sister Tethys, Oceanus fathered the Okeanides, the nymphs who inhabited fountains and springs, the Nephelai, or clouds, and the Potamoi, gods of the rivers. Some versions of the Greek creation story reveal Oceanus as declining to participate in the plot against Uranus.

Tethys was the wife of Oceanus and mother to his children. She was also the goddess fresh water. Often accompanied in Greek artwork by Eileithya, the goddess of childbirth, Tethys is usually shown as a nondescript figure. Her name translates as "grandmother" or "nurse," and she gave birth to many river gods and water nymphs, who were nourished through the manipulation

of the water supply that coursed below the surface of the earth.

Coeus, known to the Romans as Polos, was probably the holder of the northern pillar that held the sky above the earth as his name translated from the Latin as "pole." Interpretations of his Greek function indicate that he may have been considered the axis of the heavens around which the constellations and other heavenly bodies revolved. He was also thought to have a telepathic link to Uranus and to have been associated with inquisitive minds and intellect. He was also the god of heavenly oracles. In some creation accounts, he is considered to be a minor character, although he was thought to have

ABOVE: This archetypal image shows Zeus at peace and reclining on Mount Olympus. (Public Domain)

ABOVE: The fearsome dragon Typhon is shown in the remains of this Etrurian fresco. (Public Domain)

and brought cleverness with him as well. Epimetheus possessed no common sense and was believed to have brought stupidity to mankind, while Atlas, who was destined to carry the weight of the entire planet earth on his shoulders, was patient and daring, two qualities that are valued among humans.

The Titan goddess of order, divine law, and the rules of conduct was Themis. She was given authority over the oracles and became the second Oracle of Delphi. Utilizing the voices of the oracles, she provided mankind with instruction in the interpretation of civil authority and justice and the discernment between right and wrong. She introduced the idea of offerings to the gods along with other societal and religious practices, including morality, piety, and hospitality. She became one of Zeus's brides and was sometimes depicted seated close to the later king of the gods, offering advice on matters of the law and moral conduct.

The Titan goddess Phoebe was the third Oracle of Delphi and the goddess of radiance and brightness. She possessed the gift of prophecy and was paired with her brother Coeus. Together, they produced two daughters,

Leto, who was to become a lover of Zeus and the mother of twins Apollo and Artemis, along with Asteria, known as the "starry one." Phoebe was believed by some to have refused to take part in the plot against Uranus, therefore being spared from banishment to Tartarus, and she later bequeathed her role as Oracle of Delphi to her grandson and future god of the sun, Apollo.

Mnemosyne was the Titan goddess of time, memory, and remembrance, as well as the inventor of languages and words. She was the mother of the Muses and was credited with inventing writing and speech, representing the memorization that was required to pass oral histories down through generations. Therefore, she was essential to the preservation of the stories of the gods and their rise to power and conflict. As a minor oracle, she was possibly a forerunner of the nine daughters of Zeus, who were the goddesses of music.

The Titan Rhea became the wife of her brother, Cronus, and served as the figurative mother of the gods. In that role she was goddess of all motherhood and female fertility. As her name translates from Greek as "flow" or "ease," it was probably related to the process of birth. She also served as representative of time and events. She was the mother of Cronus's children, and both remembered the prophetic warnings of Uranus and Gaia.

Although he fathered many children, Cronus was determined not to allow his own offspring to threaten his hold on power. And so, as each of the couple's first five children, Hestia, Demeter, Hera, Hades, and Poseidon, were born, Cronus gobbled them up. The spectacle of Cronus devouring her children unnerved Rhea, and she fled to a cave within Mount Ida on the island of Crete to give birth to her sixth child, Zeus. It is possible that she was assisted in her flight by both Uranus and Gaia. To deceive Cronus, Rhea brought him a stone wrapped in baby clothing. Without looking at it, Cronus abruptly swallowed the stone. With

the deception complete, Zeus was raised in safety on Crete.

The infant Zeus was primarily cared for by Amalthea, known as the tender goddess and foster mother, who is usually shown in the figure of a goat or a goat tending to a nymph. Nourished by Amalthea's milk, Zeus grew strong as his cries were muffled by the Curetes, demi-gods whose dancing was complemented by the clanging of their spears and shields. Cronus, then, could not hear any noise that would give away the presence of his sixth child.

As Zeus grew to maturity and Cronus aged, the former continued the theme of conflict between father and son, conspiring to overthrow Cronus. Zeus enlisted the aid of Metis, an Oceanid and the daughter of Oceanus and Tethys. True to her name's translation as "wise counsel" or "magical cunning," Metis brought to Zeus a potion. If Cronus ingested the elixir, he would regurgitate the brothers and sisters of Zeus along with the stone that he had now carried for some time. Cronus downed the potion, and shortly afterward the plan succeeded.

The initial contents of Cronus's stomach to emerge was the stone. When he saw it, Cronus immediately knew that he had been duped by Rhea years earlier. The prophecy of Uranus had been fulfilled. After the stone came the five gods and goddesses who were destined to live on Mount Olympus and rule there with their wise brother. These included Hera, queen of the gods, Poseidon, god of the sea, Hestia, goddess of the hearth, Demeter, goddess of crops and the harvest, and Hades, god of the underworld. Some accounts relate that Hades did not reside on Olympus, but rather in the underworld.

Father and son, Cronus and Zeus, then went to war for the coveted throne of the gods. A decade of conflict followed as Zeus battled Cronus and the Titans. The Titanomachy, as the war was called, was believed to have been fought in Thessaly.

ABOVE: Zeus and Hera feast with the pantheon of gods on Mount Olympus. (Creative Commons Rijksmuseum)

ABOVE: Zeus holds lightning bolts in his fist while doing battle with Typhon. (Public Domain)

RIGHT: After terrible conflicts, Zeus emerged victorius as king of the gods on Mount Olympus. (Public Domain)

Фиг. 11.

In the midst of the fighting, Zeus was urged by his grandmother, Gaia, to free the Hecatonchieres and the Cyclopes from exile in Tartarus in exchange for their help in the fight.

Zeus addressed the Hecatonchieres, "Brothers, I seek your help in battle, and for your services I will set you free. But beforehand, you must prove that you have mastered the use of your limbs as well as your rage. I give you three tasks to prove you are worthy of your freedom."

The Hecatonchieres, said Zeus, were to vanquish Campe, the dragon which guarded the entrance to their prison in Tartarus. Next, they were to hurl a boulder to the top of Mount Olympus, and third they had to locate the Cyclopes and assist them in making weapons that would finally end the war with Cronus in victory.

With the tasks accomplished, the Hecatonchieres threw large boulders at the Titans, while the Cyclopes fashioned powerful lightning bolts and thunder that Zeus employed against Cronus. Although the majority of the Titans supported Cronus, some accounts of the war assert that Themis and her son Prometheus supported Zeus and the Olympians. Others say that Prometheus stayed out of the conflict. The brothers and sisters of Zeus, Hera, Hades, Poseidon, Hestia, and Demeter, did assist him in the war against Cronus.

When the victory was secured, Zeus imprisoned the Titans in Tartarus and posted the Hecatonchieres as guards to keep them locked up. Many years after Zeus had firmly established his reign over the universe, he freed the Titans and granted Cronus rule over the Elysian Islands, believed by the Greeks to be the place where the "blessed dead" resided.

Even after a period of relative tranquillity and the Olympian gods had taken up residence in their home high on Mount Olympus, threats to the reign of Zeus emerged. Gaia was believed to have been severely angered with the defeat of her children, the Titans, and attempted to avenge them. She summoned Typhon, or Typheous, her last child and also the son of Tartarus, another of the primordial gods. Depicted as creation's most powerful monster, Typhon was a fire-breathing dragon that never slept. Its 100 heads were menacing, and in battle the dragon wounded Zeus, tearing tendons from his body.

Hermes interceded, restoring the severed tendons and renewing Zeus's strength. Zeus then vanquished Typhon with his powerful lightning bolts and imprisoned the fearsome dragon beneath Mount Etna, the legendary volcano on the eastern coast of Sicily.

Afterward, another threat arose when the Giants rebelled against the Olympian gods. The Giants were supposedly invincible as long as their feet remained on the ground, and in their number was Endeladus, who was defeated by Zeus and sent to join Typhon beneath Mount Etna. The youthful Mimas threw large boulders and burning trees at the Olympian gods, but his demise came either as Hephaestus hurled huge shards of glowing hot metal at him or as he was destroyed by thunderbolts from Zeus.

Finally, when peace was restored, Zeus, the great victor after three stern tests in battle, was firmly established as king of the gods. However, he became his own worst enemy. Although he displayed admirable traits of courage and determination that the

ABOVE: Zeus, king of the gods and master of the skies, is shown in this statue.

(Creative Commons Mario Leonardo Iniguez via Wikipedia)

ancient Greeks hoped to emulate, he was also prone to base emotions and actions that engendered the mistrust of his wife, Hera.

Hesiod's story of the origin of the gods laid the foundation for the pantheon of Olympian deities and lesser immortals with which modern Western civilization is most familiar. He was the first known author to place himself within a written work with active voice. Believed to have been born in Boetia in central Greece, he was said to have begun his poetic career after being visited by the Muses while tending sheep.

Along with Hesiod's account of creation, other alternative visions were known to the ancient Greeks. One of these is attributed to the Pelasgian civilization, a forerunner of ancient Greece. Their version states that Eurynome, goddess of all things, was responsible for creation. She was born of Chaos and then separated the sky from the waters, dancing naked across the waves and always quickening her pace, catching the wind in her hands and rubbing it into the form of the serpent Ophion. The snake became enamoured of Eurynome and wrapped itself around her seven times.

Their close contact conceived the universal egg, and Eurynome told Ophion to coil around the egg seven times. When the egg hatched, the earth and everything in creation emerged. Afterward, Eurynome ascended to Mount Olympus to watch creation mature. The serpent joined her but began to boast that he alone was responsible for creation. For his impudence, Ophion was ejected from Olympus. Eurynome then created the planets and the moon, giving the Titan gods rule over them. Cronus and Rhea were given the planet Saturn. Ironically when compared to Hesiod's story of creation, they were also given the power of peace.

The ancient Greeks accepted the varied stories of creation and the origin of the gods, turning their attention to those who prevailed amid great trials, worshipping and constructing great temples to the glory of their contemporary gods – and turning their eyes toward the imposing heights of Mount Olympus.

MYTH OF MOUNT OLYMPUS

On the frontier of Macedonia and Thessaly, Mount Olympus, the tallest peak in Greece, soars 2,918 metres (9,573 feet) above sea level. For the ancient Greek peoples, the heavens and the earth met at the foot of the great mountain.

Olympus was the dwelling place of Zeus, king of the gods, and the Olympians, the favoured 12, including Hera, queen of the gods and goddess of marriage and birth; Apollo, god of the sun, light, truth, and healing; Artemis, twin of Apollo and goddess of the hunt, chastity, virginity, and the moon; Athena, goddess of wisdom, reason, and literature; Demeter, goddess of corn, grain, and the harvest; Hermes, winged messenger of the gods; Hestia, goddess of the hearth; Ares, god of war; Aphrodite, goddess of love, beauty, sexual pleasure, and fertility; Hephaestus, blacksmith of the gods; and Poseidon, god of the sea and brother of Zeus according to some sources.

These were the principal gods among the pantheon of deities worshipped by the Greek peoples, and at the base of Olympus lived the nine muses, the inspirers of music, literature, art, and science.

ABOVE: The gods participate in a celestial feast in this painting from 1623 by artist Cornelius van Poelenburgh. (Public Domain)

ABOVE: Apollo meets two muses, who reside at the foot of Mount Olympus in this 18th century painting. (Public Domain)

RIGHT: Zeus and the gods of Olympus gather around a chess board, possibly to make moves in the affairs of mortals. (Creative Commons Metropolitan Museum of Art via Wikipedia)

Mount Olympus becomes prominent in Greek mythology during the struggle between Zeus and his father, Cronus, and the Titans for dominion over the heavens and the earth. The bitter war, known as the Titanomachy, lasted for 10 years. Eventually, Zeus and his allies were victorious over the older generation of gods. The role of Mount Olympus varies a bit from one ancient account of the war to another. Some report that Olympus served as the base of operations for Zeus, while others assert that the high mountain became his home after the conflict had ended.

In either case, the status of Mount Olympus and the victory of Zeus and the "Olympians" was significant for Greeks in that it signified the emergence of a new generation of gods, possibly more enlightened but nevertheless exhibiting faults and character flaws that were ever present in the human condition as well. Thousands of Olympian gods were believed to be imbued with certain capabilities — powers that exceeded those of mere mortals in some respect and maintained or reinforced earlier concepts of creation and human

existence. The gods further supported the archetypal Greek ideal that the advancement of civilization is achieved through recurring struggle.

While some sources state that Zeus made his home on the actual summit of Olympus, others relate that his abode was in the heavens, high above the physical mountain. In either case, its grandeur, no doubt, was in keeping with the status of the residents. The abode of the gods was enclosed by a pair of golden gates fashioned by Hephaestus, or in some accounts by gates of clouds. The Horai, or

ABOVE: Artist Domingos Sequeira painted this image of gods in the heavens above Mount Olympus in 1794. (Public Domain)

ABOVE: The gods of Olympus enjoy their magnificent surroundings in this 16th century painting by Maarten van Heemskerck. (Public Domain)

Seasons, stood beside these gates as sentinels. Early Greek historians describe the palace as an acropolis or citadel that gleams in the distance, and depending on the source consulted, the other gods that dwelled on Olympus either lived communally with Zeus or in lavish palaces of their own featuring foundations of bronze with walls and fixtures of marble and gold. The palaces were also the handiwork of Hephaestus, the son of Zeus and Hera, or as some have opined, the son of Hera alone.

Of course, the focal point of Olympus was the awe inspiring palace of Zeus. Its adornment included an expansive courtyard with many covered passageways leading to it, allowing room for all the other gods, demigods, and immortal lesser beings to congregate when Zeus called a meeting. The centre of the palace was the main hall with flooring of gold, where feasts, celebrations, and performances were held, as well as debates and discussions that were often lively and contentious. Zeus provided his guests with opportunities to view events taking place on earth while they were in the palace. He entertained himself by allowing a clear view or obscuring some of the details of the activities far below as he deemed fit. Living quarters and storage areas lined the sides of the great hall, and there have been mythological allusions to a second palace with access restricted only to Zeus. From

the solitude of this height, he surveyed all activity going on below.

The throne of Zeus was described in detail by British poet and author Robert Graves in his 1955 two-volume compendium of Greek mythology. Graves wrote that the throne was located at the end of the large hall within the palace. Seven steps of different colours rose to the seat itself, wrought by Hephaestus of course, in black marble from Egypt with adornment of gold. The symbol of Zeus, a golden eagle, its eyes inset with rubies, sat on the right arm of the throne with strips of tin pouring from its mouth to symbolize the powerful lightning bolts for which he was known. A bright blue canopy stretched above and mimicked the majesty of the sky, while a purple ram's fleece was draped across the seat and used to make rain.

Graves further wrote that Hera's throne was beside Zeus's and accessed by three steps of crystal. The throne was carved of ivory and decorated with cuckoos in gold. The full moon was fixed above, and Hera used a white cowhide to conjure rainfall.

Though the work of Graves has been praised and ridiculed, it is probably more his own interpretation than the result of researching ancient works. Nevertheless, its vivid description is entertaining and seems fitting – that is, worthy of the gods.

Hades, god of the underworld and brother of Zeus, did not reside on Mount Olympus. The explanation offered by some historians for this is the settlement reached by the three brothers, Zeus, Poseidon, and Hades, after the victory over Cronus and the Titans. The trio met to discuss the disposition of the spoils, that is, the heavens, earth, and the underworld. They cast lots, and Zeus won big. He became supreme ruler of earth and sky, along with the sea that was placed in Poseidon's trust, and the underworld, the abode of the dead, where Hades was destined to rule beneath the earth.

Curiously, there is some discrepancy as to whether Hestia did actually reside on Olympus. One of the original 12 Olympian deities, she was the daughter and first-born of Cronus and Rhea, who was both his wife and older sister. Hestia is at times remembered as being somewhat lower in status than the other gods of Olympus, and she was prohibited from participating in some of the great celebrations and festivals that took place on the high mountain. Rather than ornate, her throne was simple and constructed only of wood.

Some historians believe that Hestia gave up her place among the 12 Olympian gods and allowed Dionysus, god of wine, winemaking, and fertility, to take her place. Her gesture may have been intended to maintain the peace on Olympus, since Dionysus was the son of Zeus and a mortal woman, Seleme. Still, some evidence suggests that the ancient Greeks were divided in their acceptance or rejection of this story of Hestia. Although the frieze on the east wall of the Parthenon shows Dionysus taking his place among the favoured 12, Hestia is present at the altar to the Olympian gods in the agora of Athens.

The gods of Olympus lived leisurely, socializing, observing the activities of the humans below, plotting and scheming, and feasting on nectar and ambrosia, the mythological food and drink of the gods. Their sustenance was delivered to them by doves, and its potency was beyond that of ordinary food while its aroma was tantalizing.

However, for all its wonder, the seemingly idyllic existence of the Olympian gods was sometimes challenged and even fraught with intrigue. And the mortal Greeks gazed upon the enduring heights.

ABOVE: Mytikas, the highest peak of Mount Olympus, reaches skyward on the frontier of Macedonia and Thessaly. (Creative Commons stefg74 via Wikipedia)

GREEK MYTHOLOGY AND MODERN INTERPRETATION

Although mankind has been fascinated and inspired by Greek mythology for thousands of years, its tales of gods and demigods, adventure and intrigue providing entertainment, relatively little exploration of its origin or its interpretation took place until the Age of Enlightenment. Acknowledging that Western civilization was directly descended from ancient Greece, it followed that scholars of the period would see mythology as a thread within the fabric of centuries of cultural development.

The awakening was largely spurred by German scholars, including Johann Matthias Gesner, a professor at the University of Göttingen, who offered a study of Greek mythology and culture in the early 1700s. As successor to Gesner, Christian Gottlob Heyne brought science into Greek studies with in-depth translations of early works, the introduction of archaeology, and the study of oral and written language to determine histories, origins, and early meanings – better known as philology.

This academic awakening spread and fostered a renewal of interest in Greek mythology during the period, and Heyne was indeed a catalyst for that new energy. Another German scholar, Johann Joachim Winkelmann, brought art into the equation and was the first to classify Greek, Greco-Roman, and Roman styles while assigning time periods to each. Consequently, he intertwined the study of Greek mythology,

ABOVE: Johann Matthias Gesner studied Greek mythology at the University of Göttingen in the 1700s. (Public Domain)

which inspired much of the art he was already evaluating. His 1755 work Thoughts on the Imitation of Greek Works in Painting and Sculpture sparked a surge of interest in Greek mythology across Europe.

Common elements in Greek and other Indo-European languages intrigued Max Müller, a German-born scholar who lived most of his life in Britain. During the mid-1800s, Müller translated ancient Sanskrit texts, many of which were brought to Britain by the East India Company, and noted that these texts, particularly the Rig-Veda, held some critical details in the development of pagan religion in Europe. He saw the gods depicted in the Rig-Veda as offspring of human explanations for the forces of nature and naturally occurring phenomena. It followed that the pantheon of Greek gods shared that origin.

Müller had discovered common themes in myths and subsequently in the development of both religion and culture. He concluded that the human mind responds in certain ways to external phenomena in order to rationalize the world in which we live.

In 1871, English cultural anthropologist Edward Burnett Taylor published a two-volume work titled Primitive Culture, which

laid the foundation for the expansion of cultural anthropology. He reasoned that three stages define any society – savagery, barbarism, and civilization. With the goal of perhaps offering betterment to British society, he asserted that cultural development across millennia has led to uniform action due to uniform causes while laws of human thought and action have existed since earliest times.

Following along with Taylor and others, American Joseph Campbell, a professor at Sarah Lawrence College in New York, considered the archetypal hero and accompanying themes that are found throughout Greek mythology. In 1949, his book *The Hero with a Thousand Faces* traced a common pattern that exists across time and transcends cultural barriers. At the same time, Polish scholar Bronislaw Malinowski concluded that mythology satisfies a basic human need, a common belief system. In turn, that system is essential to cultural and societal cohesion and identity.

In the 20th century, French anthropologist Claude Levi-Strauss looked at the theory of structuralism, which reasons that components of a culture are understood best in the context of the overall human experience and attempts to describe the framework that guides human interaction and the individual interpretation of the world around us.

BOVE: German scholar Max Müller linked Greek mythology to Indo-European tradition. (Public Domain)

ABOVE: Edard Burnett Taylor looked for common cultural development across civilization and the passage of time. (Public Domain)

ABOVE: Sigmund Freud viewed mythology in the context of psychoanalysis and the interpretation of dreams. (Public Domain)

Levi-Strauss published two landmark works regarding structuralism and his theory that the civilized mind and the savage mind exhibit the same human characteristics. His 1962 book *The Savage Mind* discusses primitive thought that includes common experiences and ideas that reside with all human beings regardless of their external environment. Published in four volumes, his 1971 book *Mythologiques* follows a single myth that began at the tip of South America and its journey across years to Central America and then to the Arctic. Therefore, he established the common link that proved his theory. So, it is not a great stretch to apply the same logic to Indo-European culture giving rise to the later Greek mythology.

The famed father of psychoanalysis, Sigmund Freud, tied the understanding of the symbolism of Greek mythology to the regular functioning of the human psyche. He contended that myths were the manifestations of repressed desires, thoughts, or ideas and commented that interpretation of dreams could provide the foundation for understanding the origin of a particular myth.

Swiss psychiatrist Carl Jung, a contemporary of Freud, explored the concept of the collective consciousness and the timeless character types it engenders. He asserted that mythology was more a product of the human mind than an interpretation of the physical world or an attempt to prove the existence of a god or multiple gods and that mythology must be read and understood through its underlying symbolism.

Like much of Western society, the Christian church has long viewed Greek mythology as fable or quaint fiction, and in fact the word "myth" has held that

meaning for many. For at least half a millennium Christian theologians reasoned that mythology was archaic and harmful to the furtherance of Christian teachings. In a broader sense, however, mythology may convey a religious concept or truth in a language or presentation more easily understood by the common people.

Some 20th century scholars have seen mythology as a contributor and essential component of the human experience, even reasoning that mythology is in fact the foundation of religion. J.R.R. Tolkein, author of the immensely popular Lord of the Rings and The Hobbit, was a devout Roman Catholic who remarked that mythology was "a divine echo of truth" and even a "subcreation" within the primary creation of God.

Author C.S. Lewis, urged by his friend Tolkein to return to the Christian church after leaving the institution, has become well known for his works that include the Chronicles of Narnia, a popular series of seven fantasy novels for children. The series incorporates characters from Greek and Roman mythology, fairytales emanating from the British Isles, and Christian themes and teachings.

When asked about the nature of Christianity, Lewis called the story of Jesus Christ a "true myth." He explained that Christ's life, death, and resurrection drama is "a myth working on us in the same way as the others, but with this tremendous difference that it really happened, and one must be content to accept it in the same way, remembering that it is God's myth where the others are men's myths: i.e. the pagan stories are God expressing Himself through the minds of poets, using such images as

ABOVE: Famed author J.R.R. Tolkein called mythology a 'divine echo of truth.' (Public Domain)

He found there, while Christianity is God expressing Himself through what we call real things."

Modern Christian teachers and theologians hold varied perspectives on the consistent and literal interpretation of the Bible text and the existence of allegorical or mythical elements in the scriptures. Some offer that Christianity does maintain historical links to ancient Greek religion and other religions of the world through shared or similar stories or, perhaps, myths.

Today, elements of Greek mythology are ingrained in society. Language, film, art, architecture, and literature are replete with such references. Western civilization continues to mature amid its influence.

ABOVE: In this 1917 photo of University College, Trinity undergraduates, C.S. Lewis stands at far right. He saw mythology in a Christian context. (Public Domain)

THE CLASSICAL PERIOD

To borrow a phrase from author Charles Dickens, the Classical Period of ancient Greece may truly be characterized as both the "best of times and the worst of times."

The Archaic Period set the stage for Classical Greece. The city state, or polis, was firmly established. The Iliad and the Odyssey of Homer, great works of literature that told the epic stories of Mycenaean heroes and their struggles with men and gods, became the basis of religious practice and gave the Greeks of the Classical Period a sense of themselves, their place in the world, and their destiny to become a great civilization.

Generally dated by historians from 480 BC, the sack of Athens and the naval victory at Salamis, to 323 BC and the death of Alexander the Great at the age of only 32, the Classical Period spanned the height of Greek cultural achievement and the depths of continuing war and political intrigue. During the period, the city states were fighting the external threat of the Persian army under Xerxes or fighting with one

another. The latter circumstance brought on the devastating Peloponnesian War, which left Sparta victorious but in no shape to establish a firm dominion.

Athens and Sparta did rise to pre-eminence as the awakening of the Archaic Period led to the flowering of the Classical. However, their inherent mistrust of one another spelled their eventual downfall. In the meantime, the external threat of Persian domination was too great for Athens to ignore. The colonization of Ionia by Athenian settlers meant that the kinsmen of Athens were in peril when Xerxes moved militarily, a decade after the defeat of his father, Darius, and the Athenian sense of duty and adventure prevailed.

When Xerxes sought retribution against the Athenians and invaded, the war that resulted shaped Western civilization for all time. The victory at Salamis enhanced the prestige of Athens 10 years after the incredible defeat of the Persians at Marathon. The goodwill that had developed as the city states banded together in common

ABOVE: The Temple of Athena Nike was among those that rose on the Acropolis in the Classical Period.
(Creative Commons Steve Swayne via Wikipedia)

cause was fleeting. Western history extols the virtues of Leonidas and the Spartan 300 at Thermopylae. The Western psyche maintains a close attachment to the sense of duty and honour engendered.

Still, the city states, though of Greek heritage and sharing much in common, were vastly different. Sparta was a closed and militaristic society ruled by a powerful oligarchy that rigidly enforced custom and practice. The Spartan state was supreme, and individual rights and perspectives were secondary to its welfare.

At the same time, Solon, Cleisthenes, and Ephialtes sowed the seeds of Athenian democracy, wresting control of government from the hands of the affluent few and demonstrating the blueprint of representative rule for the future. Under Pericles, the golden age of Athens flourished. The great construction project on the Acropolis was undertaken around 447 BC, and the Parthenon still evokes tremendous emotion and respect for the grandeur that was Classical Athens.

The theatre flourished in Athens as the Greek tragedy became prominent with

ABOVE: The Persian King Xerxes flew into a rage with the defeat of his navy at Salamis. (Public Domain)

ABOVE: The great philosopher Socrates teaches in ancient Athens. (Public Domain)

the works of Sophocles, Aeschylus, and Eurypides. The comedy was exemplified in the biting satire of Aristophanes. The philosophical schools of Socrates, Plato and Aristotle expanded the contemplation of the human condition, arousing both discovery and controversy. Even now, the basis of Western thought and culture resides in the perspectives of these great thinkers. Several differing philosophical schools emerged in the years after Socrates, including Stoicism, Skepticism, Cynicism, and Epicureanism.

The soaring art of Classical Greece was reflected in its architecture, literature, music, and the work of skilled artisans and craftsmen. In the representation of the human form, Classical Greek art takes a much more decided approach toward the form of the human body. Rather than simply alluding to it, the form exists in more direct representation. The faces are expressive and representative of logic over emotion as mankind becomes the focus of thought and exploration. Movement away from the ideal to the realistic led to a new focus on the representation of human beauty and experience, even in depictions of the mortal or of the divine gods of Olympus.

Hippocrates became the father of modern medicine, and his oath is repeated to this day. Discoveries surrounding the physical nature and the function of the body set early standards for advances in medicine. Scientific discovery flourished, opening the door to the broader contemplation of everything from the biological to the cosmos.

The discovery of silver in the mines near Athens produced great wealth, and the subsequent prosperity served as a catalyst for the surge in cultural development. Paradoxically, it also facilitated the construction of the Athenian navy, under the direction of Themistocles, which won the victory over the Persians at Salamis and preserved the city state despite the fact that the Persians sacked Athens and put the Acropolis to the torch. Even as Xerxes

ABOVE: Spartans and Thebans clash during their devastating war of the Classical Period. (Public Domain)

withdrew and the army he left behind was defeated at Plataea, ending the threat of subjugation to the Persians, Athens and Sparta were again on a collision course.

Pericles led Athens as the "First Man" of the city for three decades, facilitating the cultural awakening while also refusing to forge a lasting peace with Sparta. Following the Second Persian War, Pericles established the Delian League, which more or less became an Athenian empire rather than a congress of equals. The economic strength of the Delian League, the hegemony of Athens in the Aegean and into Asia Minor, and the potential for Athenian expansion were perceived as threats by the Spartans.

The resulting Peloponnesian War crippled the city states. Athens was defeated, and Pericles died in the great plague that swept through the city. While the Spartans were ferocious warriors, their administrative capabilities proved inadequate. Their ability to govern was tenuous as wars were fought with other Greek city states. Thebes had always been troublesome, for example, and the Spartan-Theban War of 378 BC to 362 BC raged, the Thebans actually winning a great military victory at Leuctra in 371 BC and a few years later at Mantinea that left Sparta permanently weakened. The Athenians took advantage of Spartan distraction and picked up the pieces of their broken society. They rebuilt their destroyed city and fielded a new army while a new navy was constructed.

Still, the city states had been left vulnerable by the years of internal strife. To the north lay the burgeoning power of Macedonia and its adventurous King Philip II. He moved southward and defeated the Athenians and an alliance of the city states that notably did not include Sparta, at the Battle of Chaeronea in 338 BC. Philip managed to assert control over northern Greece and within two years much of the remaining Peloponnese and Attic peninsulas were in Macedonian hands. His assassination in 336 BC led to the ascendance of his son, Alexander the Great.

The Classical Period, therefore, exemplified the heights of human achievement and aspiration while also witnessing the destructive power of warfare driven by human pride, ambition, and desire. It was a pivotal era in human history. Beyond the conquests of Alexander, the future Hellenistic Period would extend Greek influence across the known world.

ABOVE: The Derveni Krater was fashioned by a skilled Greek artisan in the late 4th century BC.

(Creative Commons Carole Raddato via Wikipedia)

ABOVE: The Lion of Chaeronea was erected on the site of the battle with the Macedonians, probably to honour Theban warriors. (Creative Commons Philipp Pilhofer via Wikipedia)

SOCRATES

He was born circa 470 BC, the son of Sophronicus, a stone mason or sculptor, and Phaenarete, a midwife. His family was of sufficient financial means to provide for an education that was rather common among the young people of Athens. He became a well-known sculptor in his own right, and some said that his statue of the graces, which was situated along the road to the Acropolis, was admired by travellers for centuries after his death in 399 BC.

He served with distinction in the Athenian army, as a hoplite, an infantryman whose bravery was documented in saving the life of Alcibiades, commander of the Greek forces, at the Battle of Potidaea. He otherwise spent virtually his entire life in Athens during the golden age of the city's cultural awakening under the dominion of Pericles. Married to Xanthippe, he was the father of three sons, and there was little more to say. His life had been extraordinary enough for most – that is until Socrates received word that the Oracle of Delphi had proclaimed him the wisest man in the world.

Socrates had already reached middle age when his friend, Chaerephon, is said to have inquired of the oracle whether anyone was smarter. Thinking that he would disprove the assertion, Socrates devoted the remainder of his life in the effort and in doing so established himself as the "Father of Western Philosophy." Socrates left no writings of his own, and the known accounts of his life are contained in the bodies of work of two former students, Xenophon and Plato. The latter was the most famous student of Socrates, who went on to teach Aristotle, who then tutored Alexander the Great.

ABOVE: In this engraving Socrates is shown in the school of Athens accompanied by famous Renaissance figures.
(Creative Commons Wellcome Collection via Wikipedia)

ABOVE: This bust of Socrates from the 1st century AD now resides in the Louvre in Paris. (Public Domain)

ABOVE: Socrates gathers with a group of students beneath a tree and asks questions of them. (Public Domain)

Plato asserted that Socrates had shown extraordinary interest in learning as a boy and read the works of the prominent philosopher Anaxagoras, as well as becoming acquainted with rhetoric through Aspasia, the wife of Pericles. Socrates employed a method of teaching that drew conclusions from his pupils. Rather than dispensing information, he asked a question, such as "What is piety?" or "What is courage?" When the interlocutor, or the other person taking part in the dialogue, responded, Socrates would ask another question, and the process would continue until the student arrived at his own conclusion. Such an approach to learning survives today as the Socratic Method.

Although Xenophon and Plato offer somewhat differing perspectives on the life of Socrates, Plato's Dialogues probably provide the most widely accepted viewpoint along with his famous Apology, or Defence, written by Plato as Socrates's address to the Athenian jury before which he was tried, convicted, and condemned to death on charges of impiety and corruption of the youth of Athens. Some interpreters of Plato's Dialogues, both contemporary and modern, assert that Plato uses a figure named Socrates to actually promote his own philosophical ideas; nevertheless, Plato's writings remain the most widely accepted source of documentation related to the historical figure of Socrates.

While Socrates was certainly called upon the serve in the Athenian army during the lengthy Peloponnesian War, he was a popular figure when he was in the city. To many, he was an object of curiosity, perhaps physically unattractive with bulging eyes and an upwardly crooked nose. He rarely bathed and walked through the city barefoot, his long hair unkempt and scraggly. He frequently engaged in discourse in the agora, or marketplace, of Athens, questioning the young and the mature, the well-to-do and the poor, women and even slaves; he had no regard or concern for social class.

Socrates became a controversial figure in Athens as he strove to define and to live a good and virtuous life while causing others to consider their own condition. His expansion of philosophy from the contemplation of the physical world to the aspects of abstract thought, including morality and ethics, created a new and inward focus. In doing

ABOVE: This engraved likeness of Socrates, the work of artist D. Cunego, dates to the 18th century.
(Creative Commons Wellcome Collection via Wikipedia)

ABOVE: Socrates is a central figure in this detail from a painting by Renaissance master Rembrandt. (Public Domain)

so, he became a perceived threat to the status quo. Young people were prone to hear his discussions and turn to the study of philosophy, perhaps shunning other pursuits and raising questions that were answerable only through an individual's sole interpretation and response. The polytheistic society was not immune from discussion, as Socrates refers to "the god," a reference in the singular, from time to time.

It is no great leap to conclude that Socrates might captivate a young audience, particularly as they saw their elders vexed regularly while the teacher questioned them vigorously, encouraging them to think for themselves rather than conforming to societal protocol. Should such an exercise lead an individual even to question the existence of the gods themselves so be it. Piety, or Eusebia, was a traditional Athenian

ABOVE: This image of Socrates originated in the German city of Nuremburg. (Public Domain)

concept of duty or responsibility, particularly as it related to social interaction or – more broadly – a way of life. The actions of those who embraced a new perspective on morals, ethics, or religion might actually be interpreted as breaking the law.

Among the common ethical questions that Socrates posed was whether the human penchant for weakness of will, a tendency to choose the wrong course of action despite the knowledge of what is right, really exists. He reasoned that individuals do wrongly when they consider the benefits of such action to outweigh the associated cost. Therefore, he offered a consideration of personal ethics called the "art of measurement," a process of straightening the distortions that might pull the cost-benefit analysis in one direction or another.

Socrates further sought to explore the limitations of human knowledge. He averred that he actually knew nothing, but his simple awareness of that fact indeed made him wise. Plato wrote that when Socrates questioned those who were thought to be wise "…the men whose reputation for wisdom stood highest were nearly the most lacking in it, while others who were looked down on as common people were much more intelligent."

During his lifetime, Socrates became the subject of social commentary, particularly in the theatre. In 423 BC, the playwright Aristophanes introduced his play Clouds to the public, depicting Socrates as a foolish man whose teachings are used to assist another character who is in debt to use rhetorical questioning as trickery to wriggle out of making repayment. The Wasps, another play by Aristophanes, depicts generational conflict between an older and a younger man, representative of a growing restlessness among the youth of Athens sparked by Socrates's teachings.

No doubt, Socrates was a prominent citizen after his name was drawn by lot to

fill a position in the democratic assembly of Athens, the ekklesia, in 406 BC. The Peloponnesian War was raging, and Socrates was alone in his refusal to prosecute several Athenian army generals following the naval Battle of Arginusae against the Spartans. After the fighting, the crewmen from at least 25 sunken or damaged Athenian triremes were in the water but could not be rescued and ultimately drowned. Despite his stance, the generals were convicted and executed.

After the Spartan victory in the Peloponnesian War, the brief rule of the Thirty Tyrants, Spartan puppets, was marked by the arrest and execution of Leon of Salamis, who had apparently committed no crime. According to Plato, Socrates refused to participate in the unjust series of events and said in Plato's Apology, "When the oligarchy was established, the Thirty summoned me to the Hall, along with four others, and ordered us to bring Leon from Salamis, that he might be executed. They gave many other orders to many people, in order to implicate as many as possible in their guilt. Then I showed again, not in words but in action, that, if it's not crude of me to say so, death is something I couldn't care less about, but that my whole concern is not to do anything unjust or impious. That government, as powerful as it was, did not frighten me into any wrongdoing. When we left the Hall, the other four went to Salamis and brought in Leon, but I went home. I might have been put to death for this, had not the government fallen shortly afterwards."

Such conduct demonstrates the commitment of Socrates to a life of virtue. However, in 399 BC, he was accused by three men, the poet Meletus, the orator Lycon, and the tanner Anytus, of impiety. At the time, it is possible that the Athenians were attempting to rid themselves of any association with the brief rule of the Thirty Tyrants. Even though Socrates had stood against the "evil" regime, his former student,

ABOVE: In this 16th century painting Socrates is shown with his wife, Xanthippe. (Public Domain)

ABOVE: Socrates is engaged in conversation with young people of Athens in this 19th century painting. (Public Domain)

Critias, was one of the Thirty. Had Socrates corrupted Critias and facilitated his conduct? Anytus might also have accused Socrates of causing his son to stray.

The charge read, "Socrates is guilty, firstly, of denying the gods recognized by the state and introducing new divinities, and secondly, of corrupting the young."

Socrates chose to defend himself rather than following the custom of the day and hiring an advocate, a speechwriter who would craft a statement on behalf of the accused. He chose not to seek clemency and save his own life, but in Plato's Apology stated boldly, "If you put me to death, you will not easily find another who, if I may use a ludicrous comparison, clings to the state as a sort of gadfly to a horse that is large and well-bred but rather sluggish because of its size, so that it needs to be aroused. It seems to me that the god has attached me like that to the state, for I am constantly alighting upon you at every point to arouse, persuade, and reproach each of you all day long."

Although some political repercussions may have played a role in his conviction and death sentence, it seems the primary crimes of which Socrates was found "guilty" were those of thought and willingness to express nonconformist views. When asked what penalty was appropriate for his transgressions, Socrates flouted the authority of the court and suggested that he should be honoured with a great feast at the Prytaneum, a ceremonial and public building of Athens. He was defiant to the end.

After the death of Socrates, many of his students established their own schools,

the most famous of them Plato's Academy in Athens. Interpretations of Socrates's message varied widely, giving rise to debate and ever-widening contemplation of the human condition. Many of the ancient philosophical movements that came after him asserted their link to the old teacher.

Also surviving the great philosopher is the lingering attempt to fully assess his core beliefs and compare them to the available secondary sources. This so-called "Socratic Question" is likely never to be answered since the entire record of his life and times exists only in the writings of others.

ABOVE: Socrates teaches Alcibiades, a priominent military commander and politician of Athens.
(Creative Commons Marcello Bacciarelli via Wikipedia)

THE DEATH OF SOCRATES

Plato tells us that Socrates had no fear of death, and he wrote in Apology of the teacher's comments to the Athenian jury.

"To fear death, my friends, is only to think ourselves wise without really being wise," he said, "for it is to think that we know what we do not know. For no one knows whether death may not be the greatest good that can happen to man. But men fear it as if they knew quite well that it is the greatest of evils."

Standing before the court, Socrates explained, "…I do nothing but go about persuading you all, old and young alike, not to take thought for your persons and your properties, but first and chiefly to care about the greatest improvement of the soul. I tell you that virtue is not given by money, but that from virtue come money and every other good of man, public as well as private. This is my teaching, and if this is the doctrine that corrupts the youth, my influence is ruinous indeed. But if anyone says that this is not my teaching, he is speaking an untruth. Wherefore, O men of Athens, I say to you, do as Anytus bids or not as Anytus bids, and either acquit me or not; but whatever you do, know that I shall never alter my ways, not even if I have to die many times."

Socrates was convicted by a vote of 280 to 220. His execution was delayed 30 days due to the observance of a religious festival. During that time, many of his friends and followers tried to persuade him to flee Athens. He refused because he believed that such an action would be unjust and immoral. After all, he was an Athenian citizen and was obliged to obey the verdict of the jury. An escape would, he opined, repay evil with evil while probably damaging his legacy.

Plato was not present at the death of Socrates but knew others who were. He described his teacher's last day of life through the fictional character Phaedo. He said, 'You are strange fellows; what is wrong with you? I sent the women away for this very purpose, to stop their creating such a scene.

ABOVE: Followers of Socrates mourn over his corpse after his death from hemlock poisoning. (Public Domain)

ABOVE: Socrates reaches for the cup of hemlock in this famous painting titled 'Death of Socrates' by artist Jacques-Louis David. (Public Domain)

ABOVE: Socrates addresses the jury that will later condemn him to death for impiety and corrupting the youth of Athens. (Public Domain)

I have heard that one should die in silence. So please be quiet and keep control of yourselves.' These words made us ashamed, and we stopped crying."

While those around him had wailed and bemoaned the inevitable, Plato wrote, "… He appeared both happy in manner and words as he died nobly and without fear."

When the time came, a potion of hemlock was presented in a cup by the executioner. Socrates proposed a prayer to the gods that the journey on earth would continue in happiness beyond the grave. He drank the contents of the cup and then walked steadily until his feet and legs grew heavy. When that was accomplished, Socrates reclined and waited until the toxin reached his heart, stopping its steady rhythm.

Plato concluded, "Such was the end of our friend, a man, I think, who was the wisest and justest, and the best man I have ever known."

PLATO AND ARISTOTLE

ABOVE: Plato is questioned by Diogenes in this 17th century painting. (Public Domain)

Plato, probably the most influential of Western philosophers, is widely known as the famous student of Socrates.

A prolific writer, Plato left monumental works on many aspects of the human experience. They range from the perception of reality to the living of a "good" life through virtue, and to the immortality of the soul. His most famous contribution to philosophy, which translates from the Greek as "love of wisdom," is the Theory of Forms, and his works are contained in dialogues that approach broad concepts such as justice, truth, beauty, nature, and love.

In the Theory of Forms, Plato asserts that reality – the physical world – is merely a representation of the absolute. Ideas, or Forms, are the real truth, a higher domain of truth; the world as we know it provides only a reflection of the higher truth. In his Dialogues, Plato delves into the search for truth and the understanding of what is good. He sees the example of universal truth in his Theory of Forms.

In Plato's Dialogues, characters question one another regarding a particular topic, allowing the reader to determine the proper point of view. In doing so, he advances the Theory of Forms, which says that we exist in a world of sensory perception while a world of ideal forms also exists. One of his most famous examples is the allegory of the cave, in which individuals chained to a wall within a cave are able only to perceive the shadows on the wall caused by the light of a flickering

flame, which limits their comprehension of an external reality.

Socrates is the central figure in many of Plato's Dialogues, and aspects of his life, trial, apology (defence), and execution are models of prose and discourse. Some scholars assert that the figure of Socrates is utilized only to deliver Plato's own words rather than an actual depiction of the events. Nevertheless, the apology remains a masterpiece of literature and thoughtful expression. In his famous Dialogue, "Republic," the concept of justice is discussed. The formation of the perfect society, just and effective, serves as a metaphor for the perfection of the soul. Therefore, the discussion of the perfect society relates to the individual's recognition of the strongpoints and weaknesses of their own condition.

Plato was born circa 428 BC into a prosperous family of Athens. His father, Aristone, was said to be descended from the god Poseidon, while that of his mother, Perictione, was related to Solon, the lawgiver of Athens, as well as Critias and Charmides, two of the Thirty Tyrants installed by the Spartans, who ruled the city state briefly after the Peloponnesian War. Some accounts state that the name Plato was given by his wrestling coach in reference to his broad shoulders, and that his actual name was Aristocles.

As a young man, Plato is believed to have initially pursued a career in literature, possibly writing poetry and plays, as well

as politics. However, he is thought to have become acquainted with Socrates' teachings while listening to him in the agora, the marketplace of Athens. Diogenes Laertius, who wrote biographies of Greek philosophers, contended that Plato was preparing to enter a competition among tragedians when he heard Socrates teaching and promptly burned his writings. At the age of 20, he became the student of Socrates.

Following the trial and execution of Socrates, Plato is believed to have travelled extensively for a number of years, probably throughout Greece, Egypt, and Italy with three trips to Syracuse on the island of Sicily, before returning to Athens and writing his Dialogues. He then founded the Academy, the forerunner of the modern university. Following his death at the age of 80, the Academy continued under his nephew Speusippus, perhaps for another

ABOVE: Plato is shown in this detail of a painting by Renaissance artist Raphael. (Public Domain)

ABOVE: Plato and Aristotle, teacher and student, walk together. (Public Domain)

ABOVE: This seated statue of Plato, completed by sculptor Leonidas Drosus in 1880, resides in Athens. (Creative Commons C messier via Wikipedia)

millennium. In addition to Socrates, Plato was undoubtedly influenced by the theories of Pythagoras, the philosopher and mathematician who founded the Pythagorean school, steeped in mysticism and emphasizing the existence of an immortal soul. The followers of Pythagoras also adhered to the concept of virtuous living and the presence of absolute truths that were essential in such a life.

The most celebrated student of Plato was Aristotle, who went on to teach Alexander the Great at the court of King Philip II of Macedonia. Although the two titans of Western thought did not agree on every point, particularly the veracity of the Theory of Forms, Aristotle was a proponent of the pursuit of truth and living of a "good" life. The divergence on the Theory of Forms did not apparently create any friction of difficulty in their relationship.

Aristotle was born in 384 BC in Stagira, a city on the coast of the Chalcidice peninsula. His philosophical and scientific works, along with those of Plato, have profoundly influenced Western thought, from the basic contemplation of human existence to the conceptualization of the Christian and Islamic religions. Aristotle's father, Nichomachus, was serving as the physician to the court of King Philip II at the time of his birth and died when Aristotle was only aged 10. Aristotle's uncle became his guardian.

At the age of 18, Aristotle was sent to study at Plato's Academy in Athens, and he is said to have resided there for two decades. When Plato died, it is believed that Aristotle was denied the opportunity to guide the Academy because of his ties to the Macedonian ruling family. Due of

that circumstance, he journeyed to the Greek Isles where he continued study and contemplation. He was called to the Macedonian court in 343 BC to serve as Alexander's teacher, and the two formed a lasting relationship. Their association as teacher and pupil lasted seven years, and Aristotle did not return to Athens until around 335 BC.

Aristotle and Alexander remained in contact through letters, and there is evidence that the former's advice and counsel influenced the conduct of the great conqueror as the years passed. It is said that Alexander's love of literature, fostered by Aristotle, caused him to carry a copy of the Iliad during his military campaigns, and the philosopher and historian Plutarch wrote that Alexander kept the famous work by Homer under his pillow. Further, Aristotle is thought to have encouraged Alexander to wage war against the Persians.

When Aristotle returned to Athens, he established his own academy, the Lyceum. He was a proponent of the search for happiness, which he interpreted as eudaimonia, which translates literally as "to be possessed of a good spirit." Like Plato, he believed that this could be achieved through living virtuously. However, he could not reconcile an unseen force or element as the explanation for the tangible and visible existence. He reasoned that the "First Cause" was responsible for the movement of everything in the universe. The so-called prime mover caused the motion of everything in the universe but itself remained unmoved.

Aristotle, then, concluded that the description of something as beautiful lay in its attributes that humans would normally associate with the concept of beauty, not,

ABOVE: Plato is considered by scholars to be the preeminent Western philosopher. (Creative Commons Yair Haklai via Wikipedia)

ABOVE: Renaissance artist Raphael depicted Aristotle in his painting of the School of Athens. (Public Domain)

as Plato had said, as it related to a realm of perfect beauty. Subsequently, he became the first philosopher to develop the study and application of logic. He determined that an individual lived the good and virtuous life because he was taught to do so, contradicting Plato's assertion in his Dialogue of Meno that there is no real learning, only remembrances from a past life, and therefore concept of a higher truth, as contained in his Theory of Forms, was not gained through experience.

Aristotle wrote of the "golden mean" or "golden middle way" in Book Seven of his work Nicomachean Ethics, advocating that moderation was the proper course in all things while in pursuit of the "good" life, which constituted the state of happiness that no other individual or circumstance could take away. "In regard to pleasures and pains the mean is self-control and the excess is self-indulgence," he explained. "In taking and giving money, the mean is generosity, the excess and deficiency are extravagance and stinginess. In these vices excess and deficiency work in opposite ways: an extravagant man exceeds in spending and is deficient in taking, while a stingy man exceeds in taking and is deficient in spending."

For more than two millennia, Aristotle's model of deductive reasoning held sway across disciplines, although its application in mathematics did not follow thoroughly in all endeavours. Deductive reasoning involves reaching specific conclusions based on general ideas, a top to bottom process. Aristotle acknowledged the value of its opposite, inductive reasoning, which states that general principles are derived based on particular observations – a bottom to top approach. However, he relied more heavily on deductive reasoning in acquiring knowledge. In science, that reliance was proven to have limitations.

ABOVE: Aristotle refuses a cup of poisonous hemlock in this painting from a Renaissance school of art. (Creative Commons Wellcome Images via Wikipedia)

In logic, Aristotle discussed the concept of syllogism, which relates that certain statements made will lead to certain other statements due to the realization that they must follow one another. One familiar example asserts: all men are mortal; Socrates is a man; therefore Socrates is mortal. The conclusion is logical; however, the approach is flawed in scientific analysis. Its conclusion is already implied without the exercise of the process, while the initial, or major, premise is already self-evident. Scientifically, applying syllogism might involve an incorrect major premise, such as the basis of Greek astronomy asserting that the earth is motionless and resides at the centre of the universe. But for centuries, Aristotle's favoured form of logic was regarded as supreme.

Aristotle's conclusions touched on many aspects of the human experience, and his commentary runs the gamut from biology to philosophy, science, ethics, chemistry, botany, psychology, government, history, logic, metaphysics and more. His work Politics relates to the nature and development of the state. On the Soul speaks to aspects of memory. Poetics addresses literary vehicles, form and criticism. Ethics remains a seminal work in the quest for the "good" life and was written as a guide for his son Nichomachus.

After the death of Alexander the Great in 323 BC, it appeared that Aristotle might experience a similar fate to that of Socrates. He was charged with impiety in Athens, probably due to his earlier ties to Macedonia, and fled for his life. He died at the age of 62 in 322 BC.

While the theories of both Plato and Aristotle have been praised, analysed, criticized, disproven, and even scorned, their profound influence is undeniable. Such is proven in their legacy of inquiry and discovery.

BOVE: In this painting, Aristotle teaches in the Lyceum in Athens. (Public Domain)

ABOVE: The teachings and observations of Aristotle impacted many fields of study. (Creative Commons jlorenz1 via Wikipedia)

FURTHER PHILOSOPHERS

Influenced by their teachers and contemporaries or prompted to formulate their own original perspectives, ancient Greek philosophers offered a wide range of viewpoints on the world around them and the proper way to live.

The Seven Sages of Greece, a group of esteemed intellects who lived in the 7th and 6th centuries BC, are remembered as men who were renowned for their wisdom and contributions to Greek society. They included the politicians Pittacus of Mytilene, Bias of Priene, Solon of Athens, Chilon of Sparta, and variously two of four others, Anarchisis the Scythian, Myson of Chenae, Periander of Corinth, and Cleobulus, tyrant of Lindos.

According to some records, Cleobulus was the grandfather or father in law of Thales of Miletus. Considered by scholars to be the first Greek philosopher, Thales contemplated the construction of the cosmos and concluded that water was the single common element from which everything in nature emanated. He was among the earliest to consider the forces and composition of the material world.

Successors of Thales are believed to have taught Pythagoras, who is perhaps better known for his mathematical theories. His Pythagorean school centred on the premise that the principles of mathematics rule everything in nature, and its followers believed in the immortality of the soul, reincarnation, and humane interaction with all people. They lived by strict standards of both behaviour and diet. The Pythagorean school influenced the later work of Plato.

Democritus conceived the idea of the atom, the building block of all matter. Along with his teacher, Leucippus, he said that thought was caused by the motion of

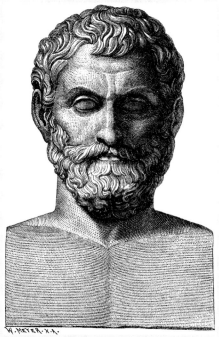

ABOVE: Thales of Miletus was one of the first philosophers in recorded history. (Public Domain)

atoms and that human souls were made up of the fire atom. He has been described as the "laughing philosopher" because of his emphasis on human happiness.

Among the first philosophers to consider human existence and thought rather than the phenomena associated with the natural world was Protagoras, who said, "Man is the measure of all things." He was an advisor to Pericles, the great leader of Athens during its flowering in the Classical Period, and his principal of Relativism stated that individual points of view dictated right or wrong while the absolute truth was unattainable.

The famous concept that earth, air, fire, and water are the primary elements that compose all matter was put forward by Empedocles, who also founded a medical school. He believed that two forces, love and strife, separated or joined the elements, while the heart was the centre of human consciousness rather than the brain.

Another pre-Socratic philosopher, Anaxagoras was convinced that the earth was formed from an infinite number of microscopic particles rather than the four elements as Empedocles reasoned. He was famous for noting that the moon was not a god and that the sun is simply a hot rock. He renounced the pantheon of Greek gods and other ideologies of his time, which prompted his conviction by an Athenian jury on a charge of atheism and led to his banishment.

A student of Thales, Anaximander became the head the school at Miletus, succeeding his teacher, and discussed a theory of eternal motion caused by opposites. Epicurus founded The Garden, a school that emphasized pleasure as the ultimate good and pain as the ultimate evil. Modest pleasure, he said, would lead to a good life. He reasoned that death was not to be feared; humans simply cease to exist because no pleasure or pain exists on the physical level or in consciousness.

Diogenes was the founder of the cynical school, proclaiming that people should live lives devoid of possessions, essentially in poverty, to free themselves of social aspirations, allowing individuals to live according to their basic, animalistic state. Zeno of Citium was the first of the Stoic philosophers, who practiced acceptance of circumstances over which individuals have no control. He developed a wide following, including the famed Roman ruler Marcus Aurelius.

Plutarch is among the most influential philosophers who lived under Roman rule. He sharply criticized the writings of the historian Herodotus, and the collection of essays titled Moralia, related to Greek and Roman life and morality, is attributed to him.

Of course, many other Greek philosophers espoused opinions and perspectives on the physical and the metaphysical; these are but a few of many such well-known figures.

ABOVE: Accompanied by representative dogs, Diogenes sits in the tub he calls home and lights a lamp to search for a proverbial 'honest man.' (Public Domain)

ABOVE: Empedocles emphasized the elements of earth, air, fire, and water. (Public Domain)

HERODOTUS AND HISTORY

ABOVE: Herodotus, author of Histories, is remembered as the Father of History. (Public Domain)

Herodotus, author of the seminal work Histories, was called the "Father of History" by the Roman orator and statesman Cicero. It is Herodotus, whose chronicle of the Persian Wars and the context in which they occurred, that has provided the Western world with the vivid descriptions of the Persian Empire, the Greek peoples who opposed invasion and subjugation, and the experience of individual combat during ancient times.

Although his work is read as history, there is no doubt that Herodotus embellished his accounts from time to time. It appears that he may have been as much a storyteller as historian, realizing that his audience would be captivated by great tales of heroism and intrigue rather than a simple recitation of the facts as he knew them. Critics have gone as far as to call Herodotus the "Father of Lies" as well. However, such criticism may well be too harsh given that the definition of a history in his time seems to indicate "study" or "investigative process" that may or may not be wholly accurate in its presentation.

Nevertheless, the descriptions of the Greek world view and the perspective with which they saw the Persian threat provide valuable insights for modern readers. Although some of Herodotus's contentions must be understood as fiction or hyperbole, the historical value of Histories remains. Divided into nine books by scholars of a later period, Histories contains accounts of the background of the Persian Wars along with the invasion of the mighty host under King Xerxes, and the pivotal battles of Salamis, Plataea, and Mycale that ensured Greek freedom from Persian domination. Herodotus relates the context of the first invasion that culminated with the Athenian victory at the Battle of Marathon and describes the growth of the Persian Empire, as well as going into great detail to stress the composition of the Greek and Persian armies.

Herodotus does not assert that his work is inspired by the gods or any other source than himself. Relying on the available oral recollections and his own experiences, he produced a work in which he took great pride. In the opening pages, he states, "In this book, the result of my inquiries into history, I hope to do two things: to preserve the memory of the past by putting on record the astonishing achievements both of our own and of the Asiatic peoples; secondly, and more particularly, to show how the two races came into conflict."

His style is engaging, and his use of first person narrative, while inserting dialogue into the text, and repeating great orations and speeches as he understood them provide a basis for future historical storytelling that remains popular today. As a historian, although his descriptions of places and events may well

ABOVE: This image of the building of the pyramids illustrates and edition of Histories. (No Restrictions via Wikipedia)

ABOVE: This illustration of a royal procession is found in an early 20th century edition of Histories. (No Restrictions via Wikipedia)

ABOVE: This statue of Herodotus stands along the balustrade in the Library of Congress in Washington, DC. (Public Domain)

be less than pure and thoroughly accurate, Herodotus provided a groundbreaking work that extended beyond the scope of his predecessors. These individuals had written of the history of a city, events of a confined or local nature, travelogues, and such. Herodotus, however, became the first Greek or Western historian to create a work that presents history as a whole, sweeping interaction woven together in organic form.

Herodotus was born in the city of Halicarnassus, an Anatolian city that was at the time part of the Persian Empire. The exact dates of his birth and death are not known. It is estimated that he was born around 485 BC and died approximately 420 BC. It is believed that his family was quite prosperous. Evidence to support this assertion exists in his ability to write. The eloquence of his prose indicates that he was well educated. When he was a boy, his family apparently fled Halicarnassus to the island of Samos to escape the tyranny of the oppressive ruler Lygdamis. Herodotus learned the Ionian dialect of the Greek language and wrote his master work in that dialect. Another indication of his family's wealth is that he is believed to have travelled extensively to Egypt, along the River Euphrates in Mesopotamia, north along the River Danube, to the cities of North Africa, through the Hellespont and into the Black Sea, and possibly to Babylon, although his description of the great city is significantly at odds with the archaeological record, indicating that his ideas of its size and grandeur were concoctions of his own imagination.

Although Herodotus clearly took liberties with fact in order to enhance a good story, he indeed provides a reliable source of information on Greek culture and the events of the subject period. To his credit, he indicates that some of the information the reader encounters is based on unverified information. And, after all, it was probably the best he could provide. He is believed to

have served in the Greek army for a time, and his descriptions of ancient combat appear remarkably accurate, told from the point of view of the foot soldier.

Criticism of Herodotus's work is not confined to the interpretation of modern scholars alone. He may have vacated Anatolia, in Asia Minor, because of contemporary criticism. An epitaph above one of his supposed resting places in Thuria reads, "Herodotus the son of Sphinx/ lies; in Ionic history without peer;/ a Dorian born, who fled from slander's brand/ and made in Thuria his new native land."

The earliest concerns apparently stem from his account of the Battle of Marathon and the credit that was due certain families of Athens in securing the great victory of the First Persian War. The Athenian general and historian Thucydides, who was believed to have been inspired to become a historian after listening to a dramatic lecture delivered by Herodotus, does later describe Herodotus as a storyteller. Thucydides was a student of rhetoric who advocated full control of the facts at hand, a divergence from the writings of Herodotus. He wrote the well-known

History of the Peloponnesian War in the 5th century BC and was later proclaimed the "Father of Scientific History."

Philosopher and historian Plutarch took Herodotus to task in the 1st century AD, writing an essay titled On the Malice of Herodotus. Plutarch's criticism includes a charge that Herodotus was not pro-Athenian enough, along with other supposed faults, such as a willingness to disparage some of the Greek states while extolling the might and grandeur of the Persian Empire. Some modern scholars have questioned the authorship of the essay, pointing to a pseudo-Plutarch. However, Plutarch hailed from the region of Boeotia, whose principal city is Thebes, and he may have taken offense at the description of Theban conduct during the Persian Wars as offered by Herodotus.

Regardless of historical interpretation and the absence of thorough accuracy, Herodotus did explore a new frontier, the aspect of more global historical context, larger than local and representative of the experience of a more comprehensive existence. His work, no doubt, opened the door to modern historical discourse.

ABOVE: Herodotus is shown in contemplation in this statue outside the Austrian parliament building in Vienna. (Creative Commons morhamedufmg via Wikipedia)

ABOVE: Activity is brisk in the Babylon marriage market; Herodotus describes Babylon in Histories, but the archaeological record seems to differ. (Public Domain)

ARISTOPHANES AND ANCIENT GREEK COMEDY

Ancient Greek comedy is one of three types of dramatic theatrical performances that developed in Classical Greece, including tragedy and the satyr play. Comedy is divided into three separate periods, Old, Middle, and New, each distinguished by chronology or some aspect of its recognized attributes. Old Comedy survives in the 11 extant works of the famed playwright Aristophanes written in the 5th century BC. Only these are known, and some of them in fragmentary form, although Aristophanes is believed to have written as many as 40 plays.

Middle Comedy has been virtually lost through the centuries, although some fragments remain and scholars at times include the last play attributed to Aristophanes, Wealth, as a bridge from Old to Middle Comedy or somewhat representative of it. New Comedy dates to the years after the death of Alexander the Great in 323 BC and courses through the years of the Macedonian rulers until approximately 260 BC. New Comedy is identifiable as comedy of manners, a type of comedy that satirizes a group – particularly of an upper social class – or situation comedy. Only fragmentary examples of Middle Comedy are known to exist, while New Comedy is best known for the authorship of Philemon, Menander, and Diphilus.

Aristophanes is the master of Old Comedy, but little is known about his personal life. He is believed to have been born in Athens around 450 BC and to have died in approximately 388 BC. Although he lived in Athens, there is some speculation that he may have hailed from Aegina, where his family owned property. His dramatic career began around 427 BC with the appearance of The Banqueteers, a satirical commentary on educational and moralistic theories that were frequent topics of discourse in the day.

Aristophanes is known for his rapier wit, sometimes salacious content, bawdiness, and irreverence. He was quite willing to take on the powerful, the philosophical, and the political issues of his time. His work relates to the ongoing Peloponnesian War, the institution of democracy, and literature. He did not hesitate to skewer public officials and perhaps even relished some backlash from the experience. One great example is contained in The Babylonians, which portrays the citizens of Athens as slaves to the fictitious Demos, a representation of the citizenry as an electoral body, and verbally attacks Cleon, a representative of the Athenian commercial class, who is presented as a warmonger and demagogue.

Cleon brought Aristophanes up on charges for the portrayal, but the penalty, if any was exacted, appears to have been lenient. Such a conclusion is borne out in the fact that Aristophanes went after Cleon again two years later when his play Knights appeared in 424 BC. Cleon is again seen as a scoundrel and the slave of Demos, who is depicted as hot tempered and stupid.

In Clouds, Aristophanes attacks the Sophists, a group of itinerant teachers and

ABOVE: Aristophanes was the leading author of ancient Greek comedy during the Old period.
(Creative Commons Alexander Mayatsky via Wikipedia)

intellects who specialized in multiple fields of study. Their modern educational methods and questioning of existing morality were fodder for the playwright's sharp criticism. The eminent Socrates is not spared, as his academy is spoofed as his is portrayed with many of the characteristics of the Sophists.

The women of Athens take over the ekklesia, the citizen assembly of Athens, in the production Women at the Ekklesia. Dressed as men, the women redistribute the wealth and property of Athens and even the availability of sex in an economic system that mimics communism.

Other works of Aristophanes include Wasps, Acharnians, and Lysistrata. Wasps is a biting criticism of the Athenian penchant for civil litigation and the citizen jurors who were paid for their service. Again, Cleon is a target for his supposed exploitation of the judicial system. Archanians is a commentary on the terrible Peloponnesian War in which the main character, Dicaeopolis, makes his own personal peace treaty with the Spartans even while being criticized for doing so. Lysistrata takes another swipe at the Peloponnesian War as the women of Athens and then all of Greece refuse to engage in marital relations with their husbands – essentially going on strike – until the war is ended. In Athens, the

ABOVE: This image from the Aristophanes play Lysistrata was taken during a 1920 performance in Germany. (Public Domain)

ABOVE: This 16th century engraving from the play Clouds by Aristophanes depicts Socrates in a basket. (Public Domain)

ABOVE: Menander was a popular playwright of the New Comedy period in Athens and across Greece.

(Creative Commons George Shuklin via Wikipedia)

women seize the Acropolis and the city state's treasury. In the end, peace is achieved.

The plays of Aristophanes combine fantasy, satire, farce, lampoon, and social commentary into a collective perspective on culture and society. He is said to have died shortly after writing Wealth, the last of his finished works that remains today. He left two more productions that were supposedly staged by his son but have been lost.

Two of Aristophanes's contemporaries were Hermippus and Eupolis. A staunch opponent of Pericles, the "First Man of Athens," Hermippus characterized Pericles as a coward and oppressor and accused his wife, Aspasia, of moral corruption and sacrilege. These attacks are believed to have occurred in his work Fates. Only fragments and titles of nine plays written by Hermippus survive.

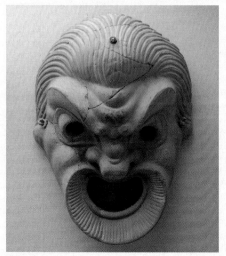

ABOVE: This ancient terra cotta comedy mask resides in a museum in Athens. (Creative Commons Jebulon via Wikipedia)

Eupolis and Aristophanes were once friends but later virulently attacked one another with charges of plagiarism. Only fragments of nine plays by Eupolis exist today.

Cratinus wrote more than 20 comedies during the Old period, and many fragments remain. His best-known work is titled Pytine, which was written in response to an unflattering criticism of him authored by Aristophanes in the play Knights. Pytine won first prize in a literary contest, besting Aristophanes' Clouds.

Middle Comedy is distinguished from Old Comedy by a reduced role for the chorus with its relevance to the plot virtually eliminated. The objects of satire in Middle Comedy are literary rather than political and more general rather than aimed at specific individuals. In Middle Comedy public figures were not personified or directly impersonated on stage. Athenaus of Naucratis, supposedly a playwright of Middle Comedy, lived in the late 2nd century and early 3rd century AD. He is said to have written on the histories of Syrian kings and on the thratta, a kind of fish mentioned in the Old Comedy work of Archippus. His work Dinner Table Philisophers is the most intact, written in 15 books that deal with various topics of the day, but little or nothing of any comedic works survives.

Representative of New Comedy playwrights, Menander wrote 108 comedies and won first prize at the Lenaia festival in Athens eight times. He was born around 342 BC and died at the age of approximately 50. His rival Philemon was born in Sicily in 362 BC, relocated to Athens, and lived to old age. Philemon is said to have repeatedly won festival prizes in competition with Menander and to

ABOVE: This figure is believed to represent a character from one of Menander's plays during the period of New Comedy. (Creative Commons Rennett Stowe via Wikipedia)

have garnered considerable popularity with his delicate wit. Diphilus was born in 342 BC at Sinope, a city on the shore of the Black Sea. He died in Smyrna in 291 BC and is known to have competed at the Lenaia festival, winning three first prizes with much of his writing involving mythical characters. He is believed to have written 100 plays with 59 titles and more than 130 fragments surviving.

AESCHYLUS, SOPHOCLES, EURIPIDES AND GREEK TRAGEDY

Greek tragedy emerged in the 6th century BC and became, along with the satyr play and later Greek comedy, one of the elements of stage performance that serves as the basis of theatre as it exists in modern times.

The origin of Greek tragedy remains the subject of debate. While some scholars have attributed its rise to an extension of the reading of epic poetry, others believe that it is directly related to religious ceremony. In his treatise on literary theory titled Poetics, Aristotle comments that tragedy began with the performance of the dithyramb, a hymn to Dionysus, the god of wine, fertility, and festivity. The complete connection between tragedy and Dionysus remains elusive; however, it is known from literature, sculpture and other artwork that such performances took place during annual festivals held in his honour.

Several theories that support the link to Dionysus include the wearing of a mask, a noted symbol of the god. The actor's wearing of the mask in turn symbolized the presence of god in man. The rituals accompanying the worship of Dionysus included animal sacrifices and the singing of a song called the "trag-odia," which may provide the origin of the word "tragedy" itself. A further link may well be found in the heavy consumption of wine during the festival of Dionysus, which might cause an individual to lose themselves with intoxication, displaying deep emotion and symbolically becoming someone else, similar to the performance of an actor.

ABOVE: The famed Greek tragedian Euripides authored many plays, but only **19** survive in complete form.

(Public Domain)

ABOVE: Aeschylus, the author of dozens of plays, is considered the 'Father of Greek Tragedy.'

(Creative Commons M.k.dionnisio via Wikipedia)

The singing and dancing that accompanied the revelry of the festival may well have given rise to the formation of the chorus, typically a group of 12 male performers wearing masks and providing context and commentary on the play as it proceeds. Its number was later increased to 15, and at times the chorus represented a particular social group, perhaps women or slaves. Sometime around 534 BC, the actor Thespis is said to have donned a mask and become first stage actor in a theatrical production, portraying a character in speech and movement, rather than speaking as himself. Actors were male, and a single actor might play more than one role, including any female.

The subject matter of Greek tragedy was derived from the mythology and tradition of the people. Therefore, religion played a central role in its development. The altar of Dionysus was located at the centre of the theatre, and the throne of the priest of Dionysus was also in a conspicuous location as he presided over the program. Great theatres that could accommodate several thousand spectators were built across Greece.

Themes included such broad concepts as honour, justice, destiny, or political power, and these were addressed with great seriousness. Often, they depicted an individual hero facing the course of events that led toward his destiny or the story of a family and its collapse due to internal or external conflict.

The Greek tragedy is composed of five elements: the hero, the tragic flaw, the catastrophe, belief in destiny, and the chorus. The hero confronts his destiny with resolve and virtue, but his tragic flaw proves his undoing to the dismay of the audience. The tragic flaw reveals the humanity of the hero who inevitably falls victim to his own judgmental error or poor decision; he cannot escape his destiny – a sorrowful, destructive end. The catastrophe reveals the terrible ending of the play, the death of the hero and the accompanying ruin. The core belief in the concept of destiny binds the audience to the drama with the understanding that the outcome has already been decided by the gods as facilitated by the tragic flaw. The chorus provides the commentary as the drama unfolds.

The production was presented in sections. The prologue provided an introduction, while the parados marked the entry of the chorus along with its identity and background information. These were followed by the presentation of episodes separated by choral music, and the exodus, the final portion of the tragedy and the ending choral song. A narrator, or witness, described events of the story that occurred offstage.

The performances of tragedies during the festival of Dionysus included competitions known as the Dionysia. Tragedians who aspired to enter a competition presented

ABOVE: The Greek tragedian Sophocles is well remembered for his tragic trilogy of King Oedipus.

(Creative Commons Wolfgang Sauber via Wikipedia)

ABOVE: An Athenian audience watches a performance of Agamemnon, a play by the tragedian Aeschylus. (Public Domain)

ABOVE: Sophocles appears second from left in this mural that also features other prominent figures of ancient Athens. (Creative Commons George E. Koronaios via Wikipedia)

their work to the archon, essentially chief magistrate of Athens or other cities where competitions were held. The archon chose the work of three authors to compete for prizes. The three plays were performed, and awards for three places were given. A fourth play, the satyr, was also performed last. Its purpose was to relate to the theme of the tragedies in the competition but also to add a lighter, more uplifting tone that would counter the sadness of the tragedies.

Greek tragedies were often written specifically for the annual competitions. Those chosen for performance during the festival of Dionysus were financially supported. The city state paid for the lead actors and the playwrights, while the archon chose three prominent citizens who would pay the costs of the chorus.

Three playwrights, Aeschylus, Sophocles, and Euripides, are remembered as the central figures of the genre. Although others were active during the period, theirs are the only works of which survive in complete form, and these are relatively few. It is

likely that the three authored more than 300 tragedies.

Aeschylus is considered by many to be the father of Greek tragedy. Born in Eleusis, a small town just north of Athens, in 525 BC, he is believed to have authored as many as 90 tragedies, but only seven are intact today. The first of the great Greek tragedians, Aeschylus is credited with adding a second character to the production, resulting in more dialogue and plot development. He also carried the theme of one play into sequels, creating the trilogy. Aeschylus died around 456 BC, and his works include the Oresteia trilogy composed of the plays Agamemnon, The Libation Bearers, and The Eumenides, as well as Seven Against Thebes, The Suppliants, and The Persians.

Sophocles was born in Colonus in 496 BC and died at the approximate age of 90. Though 118 titles of his tragedies are known

only seven are available in complete form today. Sophocles is believed to be responsible for adding a third actor to the production, again increasing the development of the plot. He introduced the use of scenery and was known to have changed scenery at times within a single play. Sophocles was immensely popular with the public, and his Oedipal Trilogy, which includes Oedipus Rex, Oedipus at Colonus, and Antigone, is still widely read today, often by literature and drama students. The other known works by Sophocles include Ajax, Electra, Trachiniae, and Philoctetes.

Euripides was born on the island of Salamis around 480 BC and died in Macedonia around 406 BC. He authored approximately 90 plays, and of these 19 have survived. Euripides was also quite popular as audiences appreciated his witty dialogue, stimulating treatment of common themes, and choral lyricism. Perhaps his most famous work is Medea, the haunting story of the title character's marriage to Jason (of Argonaut fame) and his betrayal and abandonment of her for the princess of Corinth. Medea, the former princess of Colchis, exacts terrible revenge. Euripides is also remembered for another work titled Electra, as well as The Trojan Women, Alcestis, The Bacchae, and Hippolytus.

Euripides' Cyclops is the only surviving example of a traditional satyr play. As audiences were introduced to Greek comedy, the role of the satyr play in providing comic relief was significantly diminished. Also, with the addition of actors, the role of the chorus began to fade.

Many Greek tragedies were performed again and again, their scripts copied and provided to the public, and by the 3rd century BC, theatre companies travelled to venues throughout Greece and Ionia to perform. Later, the Romans adopted the classic Greek tragedies, performing them in Latin.

ABOVE: This likeness of Euripides adorns the ceiling of the famed Apollo Theatre in Syros. (Creative Commons TakisA1 via Wikipedia)

ARCHIMEDES AND MATHEMATICS

The siege of Syracuse, founded more than 500 years earlier by Corinthian and Tenean settlers, was long and arduous. Its capture was the crowning event of the campaign for island of Sicily when Roman forces under Marcus Claudius Marcellus took possession of the city in the autumn of 212 BC. Both sides had lost heavily. Many soldiers and civilians had died, and among them was the celebrated mathematician Archimedes.

The great scholar, responsible for building mechanical weapons of war that defended Syracuse, prolonging the siege and exacting a considerable toll on the Romans, had been killed by a soldier – against the orders of Marcellus, who specified that he should live. No doubt, Marcellus knew of the mathematical skills that Archimedes possessed, and he was probably aware that the 78-year-old had devised many of the war machines that had held his legions at bay for months.

However, the story goes that Archimedes was at his residence when the strong walls of Syracuse were finally breached. He was believed to have been quietly pursuing his studies when a Roman soldier interrupted. When Archimedes abruptly told the soldier to depart from his home, the Roman – not

ABOVE: This painting depicts Archimedes, designer of several weapons systems, directing the defences of Syracuse against the Romans. (Public Domain)

knowing who the resident was – killed him without hesitation.

Born in Syracuse in 287 BC, Archimedes is remembered as the most famous mathematician of ancient Greece. Although he travelled to Egypt as a young man, he returned to his hometown and became a close friend of King Hieron II, who ruled the city state for decades. Much of his work was carried on through correspondence with other mathematicians, including Eratosthenes of Cyrene, chief librarian at the Library of Alexandria and the first person to calculate the circumference of the Earth, and Conon of Samos, a renowned astronomer who wrote De astrologia and made conclusions on the movements of stars and planets and other celestial phenomena.

Archimedes is well remembered for his discovery of the relationship between the surface and volume of a sphere within the surrounding limits of a cylinder. He was the author of a principle and resulting tool that both bear his name. The Archimedes Principle is a hydrostatic formula for raising water, and the device, which remains in use today, is known as the Archimedes screw.

During his long career, Archimedes wrote numerous treatises in the Greek language, and

nine of these are known to exist today. Perhaps his best known treatise is titled On the Sphere and Cylinder, which relates that the surface of any sphere with radius "r" is four times that of its greatest circle, or $A = 4\pi r^2$. Further, he noted that the volume of a sphere is two-thirds that of the cylinder in which it is inscribed, or $V = 4/3\pi r^3$. According to history, Archimedes took such satisfaction with the latter discovery that he provided detailed instructions in his last will and testament that his final resting place should be decorated with the etching of a sphere inscribed in a cylinder. More than

ABOVE: Archimedes is summoned to assist with the defence of Syracuse in this 18th century painting. (Public Domain)

ABOVE: A Roman soldier accosts Archimedes in his home, seconds before murdering the mathematician. (Public Domain)

ABOVE: Cicero discovers the tomb of Archimedes, overgrown with vegetation. (Public Domain)

a century after his death, the Roman senator and statesman Cicero is said to have found the tomb, neglected and obscured by plant growth.

Other known treatises by Archimedes include Quadrature of the Parabola, On the Equilibrium of Planes, On Conoids and Spheres, On floating Bodies (includes two books), Method Concerning Mechanical Theorems, Measurement of the Circle, and The Sand-Reckoner, which created a place value system of notation that allowed for the inadequate capability of the Greek numerical system to express large numbers. The treatise is written to Gelon, the son of King Herion II, and takes on the numerical expression of such infinite calculations as the number of grains required to fill the entire universe.

Measurement of the Circle is another treatise, existing today in fragmentary form, and its purpose is to show that the ratio of

ABOVE: In this engraving Archimedes uses parabolic mirrors to set fire to Roman ships during the siege of Syracuse. (Public Domain)

the circumference of a circle to its diameter, better known as π, is a number somewhere between 3 10/71 and 3 1/7. The work related to inscribing and circumscribing multisided figures, or polygons, became standard across the known world until infinite series expansions in India in the 15th century and Europe in the 17th century were in practice.

Method Concerning Mechanical Theorems, just rediscovered in the late 1800s, remains the only surviving work from ancient times that deals with a process of mathematical discovery. Archimedes describes his mechanical methodology that leads to remarkable conclusions, such as theorems applicable in determining the surface area and volume of a sphere or the area of a parabolic segment.

In reference to the life of Archimedes, more is known of his exploits than perhaps any other scientist or mathematician of ancient times. Such is probably due to the remarkable nature of the vignettes that were told and retold, fuelled by the fascination created by his considerable prowess as an engineer and mechanical wizard. After his death, Marcellus supposedly found two spheres that Archimedes had created, one a celestial globe showing positions of the stars in the sky, and the other a mechanical representation of the sun, moon, and planets. He carried both of them back to Rome, where they were objects great curiosity.

While the Archimedes screw remains one of his prominent inventions, the great mathematician was also willing to take on problems presented by others. One question that came to him was offered by his friend King Herion, who asked how much silver

and gold were contained in a wreath that had been presented to him. The anecdote relating that Archimedes determined that the answer could be found through calculations involving immersion of the wreath in water may well be fact. However, the rest of the story, which says he was sitting in the bathtub when the solution came to him and then ran through the streets naked while shouting "Eureka! I have found it!" is probably hyperbole.

The writings of later mathematicians and scientists indicate that Archimedes produced many other works in his lifetime that have been lost. Among other topics, he studied the Cattle Problem, an exercise relating to indeterminate analysis with eight unknowns, its name surviving from a Greek epigram, and he contemplated the phenomenon of refraction.

Although the contemporary influence of Archimedes' work, aside from his highly efficient weapons of war, may have been minimal, he had hoped that his discoveries would assist future inquisitive minds in advancing the scope of knowledge through their application. Translations of his works into Arabic and Latin did, centuries later, positively influence others. Works attributed to Islamic mathematicians of the 8th and 9th centuries AD may well have their roots in the labour of Archimedes. His texts are known also to have formed a basis for later achievements in the 16th and 17th centuries, including those of Galileo, Johannes Kepler, and Rene Descartes.

In addition, ancient Greek mathematicians who preceded Archimedes include Pythagoras, credited with the famous theorem regarding right triangles, $a^2 + b^2 = c^2$, and Euclid, remembered as the "Father of geometry."

The contributions of Archimedes and other mathematical scholars before and after his time are nothing short of spectacular.

ABOVE: The famed Greek mathematician Archimedes ponders a theorem while deep in thought. (Public Domain)

BELOW: The temple of Aphia in Aegina provides examples of Doric columns. (Creative Commons Alu Salt via Wikipedia)

SCIENCE, MEDICINE, AND ARCHITECTURE

The ancient Greeks were fascinated with the world around them, attributing much that they could not explain to their gods. Otherwise, they pondered a myriad of mysteries and applied the knowledge gleaned, accurate or otherwise, to their everyday lives. Advances in science, medicine, and architecture were astonishing, and their contribution to modern comprehension of the universe stands the test of time.

Throughout human existence, one of the most vexing and persistent fields of study involves individual health, the maladies that afflict mankind, and following suit, the explanation of physical infirmity and the possibilities of treatment and recovery.

Hippocrates is hailed as the "Father of Medicine." Born on the island of Cos in 460 BC, he is believed to have authored some writings on the topic during his lifetime.

ABOVE: Ionic columns are identifiable by their stylized scroll capitals. (Creative Commons Rama via Wikipedia)

RIGHT: The capitals of stately Corinthian columns are adorned with acanthus leaves.
(Creative Commons Sujay25 via Wikipedia)

ABOVE: Hippocrates, the Father of Medicine, is shown in this 17th century painting. (Public Domain)

About 60 documents which mention his name survive today, but he is not believed to have written those that are available. While it remains difficult to separate the fact and legend that surround his life in Classical Greece, it is clear that Hippocrates was revered during his lifetime. Five hundred years after his death in 315 BC, the physician Soranus wrote a biography of Hippocrates, but again the facts and fiction are inextricably interwoven.

Well known in modern medicine for the Hippocratic Oath – which he probably did not write – Hippocrates is credited with the establishment of medical ethics and standards of practice. He is believed to have travelled widely and taught extensively. His reputation grew during the Hellenistic Period, and many of the medical documents of preceding centuries were collected in the fabled Library of Alexandria as the Corpus Hippocraticum, or Works of Hippocrates.

The works were clearly written by multiple authors although they share common elements relating to such basic topics as what disease actually is, types of treatments for illnesses or conditions that were regularly seen, and discussions of recurring processes such as childbirth, along with specific writings on paediatrics and other related topics. Individual case histories are recorded along with a study of weather and seasonal changes and the correlation of emergent diseases. Among other assertions, Hippocrates proposed that diseases might be caused by poor diet; that is, undigestible foods produced toxic vapours that were pathological.

The influence of Hippocrates expanded during the Hellenistic period as knowledge increased. By the 2nd century AD, the great physician Galen credited Hippocrates with his own foundational understanding. Plato was a contemporary of Hippocrates and called him the "Asclepiad of Cos." The term "asclepiad" refers to a physician belonging to a family with a tradition of generational practitioners and is derived from the god of medicine, Asclepius.

Aristotle referred to Hippocrates as the "great physician" and offered some of his own observations regarding disease. He proposed that the human body consists of four major humours, black bile, yellow bile, phlegm, and blood. Good health was consistent with balance in these humours. Therefore, illness occurred when one or more humour was out of balance, and treatment such as bloodletting might be prescribed.

Though the future of medicine has been dictated by substantial progress in understanding, Hippocrates has remained the historical figure who blazed the trail. The comment, "Prayer indeed is good, but while calling on the gods a man should himself lend a hand," is attributed to him.

The expansion of scientific thought in ancient Greece revealed both exciting breakthroughs and miscalculations. The Greeks made little or no distinction between science and philosophy, which influenced their studies via the deductive process.

Intertwined with mathematics, astronomers plotted the paths of the moon and stars, contemplating the principles of the cosmos. Thales of Miletus is credited with the idea that the universe exists within the structure of laws of nature. In 585 BC, he accurately predicted a solar eclipse, supporting his scientific refutation of a supernatural cause and effect. Heraclides Ponticus proposed in the 4th century BC that the earth rotates on its axis. The concept that the earth orbits the sun was considered by Aristarchus of Samos in the 3rd century BC. Eratosthenes accurately calculated the diameter and circumference of the earth.

Aristotle observed the animal kingdom and classified them according to shared characteristics, authoring a book titled History of Animals. In so doing, he establish the foundation of the science of zoology. His successor in the Peripatetic School of Athens, Theophrastus, was the founder of the science of botany. Aristotle and Pythagoras also studied physics, the scientific pursuit that deals with the nature of matter and energy, performing some practical experimentation. However, the exploration of physics was most often confined to intellectual contemplation.

The ancient Greek pursuit of scientific discovery relied heavily on deductive reasoning, which had proven invaluable in mathematics. The process involves arriving at specific conclusions on the basis of general ideas, a top to bottom process. Deductive reasoning, however, is limited in application outside mathematics. Modern scientific investigation relies on inductive reasoning, the development of broad generalizations based on particular observations, a bottom to top approach, rather than the deductive method. Therefore, some contemporary scientists have seen the deductive approach as a hindrance to scientific progress at times.

The body of knowledge including mathematics, physics, and science influenced the genesis of ancient Greek architecture, whose legacy is perhaps more prominent than any other cultural aspect in modern times. The mythological figure Daedalus, honoured as an individual who embodied wisdom, knowledge, and power, was seen as a source of inspiration in craftsmanship and architecture. Daedalus is also recalled as the father of Icarus, fashioning wings and attaching them to his son with wax. In the end, according to legend, Icarus flies too

ABOVE: The Greco-Roman physician Galen conducted significant research in his field. (Public Domain)

ABOVE: Thales of Miletus is depicted in this mural at the Baths of the Seven Sages at Ostia.

(Creative Commons Institute for the Study of the Ancient World via Wikipedi)

ABOVE: The modern reconstruction of the Parthenon in Nashville, Tennessee, provides a fresh perspective on the ancient ruins. (Creative Commons White.alister.t via Wikipedia)

ABOVE: The Lincoln Memorial in Washington, DC, provides an excellent example of Greek Revival architecture. (Public Domain)

close to the sun, melting the wax and causing his fatal fall to earth.

Pheidias is often credited as the catalyst of Classical Greek architecture and sculpture. He is hailed as the designer of the great statues of Zeus at Olympia and Athena within the Parthenon. The partners Ictinus and Callicrates planned and undertook the construction of the architectural wonder of the Parthenon. Ictinus is also identified as the architect of the temple of Apollo at Bassae, and Callicrates designed the temple of Nike on the Acropolis of Athens. Theodorus of Samos, an architect and sculptor on the island of Samos in the 6th century BC, is said to have invented the processes of ore smelting and casting that became critical in sculpture, while also developing tools that have become instrumental in architecture and other pursuits, such as the ruler, key, level, and square. Dinocrates was an architect and advisor favoured by Alexander the Great. He planned the city of Alexandria and worked on remarkable temples and other structures in Delos, Delphi and other cities.

The ancient Greeks admired symmetry, and they applied their skills to produce soaring works in temples, public spaces, theatres, and other structures. Ancient Greek architecture is usually divided into three styles, or orders, Doric, Ionian, and Corinthian.

The most prominent Greek architectural achievements are in one of these three styles, particularly their magnificent temples. The great temples were characterized by their impressive colonnades. These were rows of columns in one of the three styles. Doric columns were typically simple and unadorned at the capital and base, although the columns themselves were often fluted for decoration. Doric columns were short and broad, constructed with the formula that height was six times the diameter of the base. With capitals decorated in scrolls and acanthus leaves respectively, Ionian and Corinthian columns are more ornate than Doric examples, while their height was calculated at nine times the diameter of the base.

The most famous example of Greek architecture, the Parthenon, was constructed over a period of half a century beginning in 447 BC atop the Acropolis in Athens. Its style is that of a Doric temple with additional Ionic features. It includes a portico and a colonnade on all four sides. Standing on a stylobate, or platform, with three steps, the Parthenon is constructed in post and lintel form with the columns supporting horizontal moulding and bands atop the capitals of the Doric columns. The inner chamber, called the cella, is divided into rooms. In this case, the opisthodomos, or back room, held the treasury of the Delian League. A reconstructed example of the Parthenon, visited by thousands each year, resides in Centennial Park in Nashville, Tennessee.

The influence of ancient Greek architecture in the modern world is readily apparent. The Romans admired and copied Greek architecture and other aspects of the arts and sciences emanating from their provinces in the eastern Mediterranean. Many governmental buildings around the world are constructed in Greek Revival style, reflective of an architectural movement that occurred during the late 18th and early 19th centuries. These include the façade of the British Museum in London, the Lincoln Memorial in Washington, DC, the Brandenburg Gate in Berlin, the Austrian Parliament Building in Vienna, and the St. Petersburg Bourse in St. Petersburg, Russia.

Notable inventions sprang from the Greek penchant for exploration. In addition to the machines created by Archimedes, Plato is believed to have built the world's first alarm clock, using a water clock with a trigger to chime at a certain time of day. Ancient Greek inventors built the world's first water wheel, which became an essential component in the processing of grain. Its use facilitated production that led to surpluses that fuelled commerce and trade. In order to construct many of their massive stone buildings, the Greeks invented an early crane capable of lifting tonnes of weight. Their early form of central heating used heat generated from fires, transferring the warmth beneath the floors to other areas of dwellings.

One of the world's first calculators, the astrolabe, an instrument used to make astronomical measures, is variously attributed to Claudius Ptolemy in the 2nd century AD or perhaps earlier to Hipparchus during the 2nd century BC. Even the bathtub, the hypodermic needle, the odometer, and the thermometer are said to have made their early appearances in ancient Greece.

ABOVE: The astrolabe, an early calculator used to plot movements of the stars and planets, was invented in ancient Greece. (Creative Commons Ragesoss via Wikipedia)

SUBSCRIBE

585/23

TODAY

FREE! SPITFIRE SURVIVORS SUPPLEMENT

September 2023
Issue No 605,
Vol 51, No 9

AEROPLANE
HISTORY IN THE AIR SINCE 1911

SPITFIRE SALUTE

*Celebrating
80 years of MH434...
and your guide to the
world's ai...*

Me 262...
Stunning G...
G...
Where you can le...
WAR...
Exclusive intervie...

FREE GIFT
WORTH £28.94!

Aeroplane is still providing the best aviation coverage around. With focus on iconic military aircraft from the 1930s to the 1960s.

shop.keypublishing.com/amsubs

EXCLUSIVE! 2023 ARMOUR IN THE DALES FEATURE

www.keymilitary.com

CLASSIC MILITARY
VEHICLE

September 2023 £5.80

Restored Tiger catches everyone by surprise at WWII show, but who's behind restoration?

MYSTERY AT MILITRACKS

D-Day Special
All the action from Normandy and Devon

Big Interview
Royal Tank Regiment veteran Richard Cutland

FREE GIFT
WORTH £26.94!

Classic Military Vehicle is the best-selling publication in the UK dedicated to the coverage of all historic military vehicles.

shop.keypublishing.com/cmvsubs

ng.com

CORRUPTION, CHICANERY AND RHS CHELSEA
Historic quirks from the home for heroes and its In-Pensioners

BRITAIN'S BEST-SELLING MILITARY MONTHLY

BRITAIN AT WAR

2023 ARMOUR IN THE DALES FEATURE

SPITFIRE SURVIVORS SUPPLEMENT

AEROPLANE
HISTORY IN THE AIR SINCE 1911

EXCLUSIVE HAWKER TEMPEST FIRES UP AT SYWELL

*The Home of
Aviation Heritage*

FlyPast

STORMBIRD RISING
RECREATING THE LEGENDARY Me 262

PERICLES AND THE DELIAN LEAGUE

The rivalry between the city states of ancient Greece, chiefly Athens and Sparta, inevitably led to the costly Peloponnesian War, a desperate conflict in two parts that brought Athens to its knees and so weakened Sparta that its victory led to only temporal pre-eminence in the Greek world.

Following the Greek victory in the Second Persian War, the spirit of cooperation between the city states, banded together to defeat a foreign invader, swiftly evaporated. The rivalry led to the principal city states searching the Greek world for allies. Sparta convened the Peloponnesian League along with Corinth, Thebes, Tegea, and Elis as its major allies. Conversely, Athens led the formation of the Delian League, which counted up to 330 members at its peak.

ABOVE: Pericles died during the great plague of Athens as the Peloponnesian War continued, leaving the city state bereft of effective leadership. (Public Domain)

ABOVE: Pericles is remembered as the 'First Man of Athens' and its leader during an unprecedented period of cultural expansion. (Public Domain)

Founded in 478 BC, the Delian League included numerous city states of Ionia, on the coast of modern day Turkey, as well as others along the Thracian coast and in the islands of the Aegean Sea. The Delian League continued fighting to remove Persian garrisons from Greek territory until 449 BC, even after Sparta had declined to do so.

During the years that followed, provocations were frequent as Athens and Sparta jockeyed for political and territorial advantage. Athenian domination of the eastern Mediterranean and the Aegean was a troubling prospect for the Spartans, and the considerable Athenian naval superiority in the region threatened trade with its Peloponnesian League allies. Athens was wary of the tremendous Spartan army, proven in battle against the Persians and dominant on land.

From time to time, skirmishes broke out on land and sea. Proxy wars were fought as smaller city states became entangled in disputes with one another. Negotiations were held, but neither Athens nor Sparta was completely satisfied with their outcome. Inevitably, the two coalitions stumbled toward war, and ironically the Athenian dominance of the Delian League was an eventual catalyst in the catastrophic conflict.

Pericles, a prominent statesman and general of Athens, was the dynamic presence and a driving force in the Delian League for decades during the turbulent period leading up to and including the Peloponnesian War. Athens asserted a paternalistic protectionism over the other members of the league, particularly as its strong navy provided defence against opposing Greek city states and the threat of piracy. Athens levied tribute payments from the other city states and eventually moved the nexus of league administration to the city from Delos.

ABOVE: Pericles discusses issues of the day in Athens from his sick bed. (Public Domain)

ABOVE: Pericles delivers his famous funeral oration before the people of Athens. (Public Domain)

ABOVE: Pericles mourns the death of his son during the great plague of Athens. (Public Domain)

advocate of representative government and his reforms influenced its future course. He was the catalyst for the construction of great buildings, particularly the legendary Parthenon and others of the Acropolis, and became a patron of the arts.

When he died during the plague of Athens, Pericles was approximately 65 years old. Five centuries after his death, Plutarch wrote, "This man Pericles extravagantly admired, and being gradually filled full of the so-called higher philosophy and elevated speculation, he not only had, as it seems, a spirit that was solemn and a discourse that was lofty and free from plebeian and

reckless effrontery, but also a composure of countenance that never relaxed into laughter, a gentleness of carriage and cast of attire that suffered no emotion to disturb it while he was speaking, a modulation of voice that was far from boisterous, and many similar characteristics which struck all his hearers with wondering amazement."

The name Pericles translates from the Greek as "surrounded by glory," and indeed he sought to raise the glory of Athens to new heights. It must be concluded that his effort was successful, even though the end of Athenian political primacy came a quarter century after his death.

Pericles was born into a prominent family of Athens. His mother, Agariste, was a member of the controversial Alcmaeonidae. His father, Xanthippus, had led the Athenian army to victory over the Persians at Mycale in 479 BC. According to Herodotus, days before Pericles was born, Agariste dreamed that she had given birth to a lion. Interpretations of such symbolism vary, both favourable and unfavourable. Little is actually known of Pericles's childhood and education other than his time as a pupil of Damon, a music teacher whose lessons probably encompassed a broader range of topics.

There is no evidence that Pericles was schooled in oratory; however, he undoubtedly became a public speaker of note. One interesting aspect of this talent is the belief of some scholars that his wife, Aspasia, was either his muse or actually composed many of his speeches and prodded Pericles to improve his oratorical skills. Controversy surrounds her probable influence. Pericles divorced his first wife and began a long liaison with Aspasia, who also inspired other prominent

Pericles appropriated the league treasury and brought it to Athens in 454 BC.

In regard to the antagonism with Sparta, Pericles was never in favour of negotiated settlement. Some critics have noted that his stance placed Athens on the road to eventual ruin, and some contemporaries also disapproved of the use of Delian League funds for the benefit of Athenian ventures. Truly, his political stance and leadership forged the league into what essentially became an Athenian empire. Then, with the Spartan victory in the Peloponnesian War in 404 BC, the power and prestige of Athens were broken and with that the Delian League dissolved.

However, there is no dispute that the leadership of Pericles was essential to the flowering of a golden age of Athenian culture. The historian Thucydides called Pericles the "First Citizen of Athens," and the period of his prominence, from approximately 460 BC until his death in 429 BC may rightly be characterized as the "Age of Pericles." He was a competent military commander whose oratorical skills rallied the people of Athens to new heights of achievement during roughly 30 years of authority. Although democracy had been extant in Athens, he was a vigorous

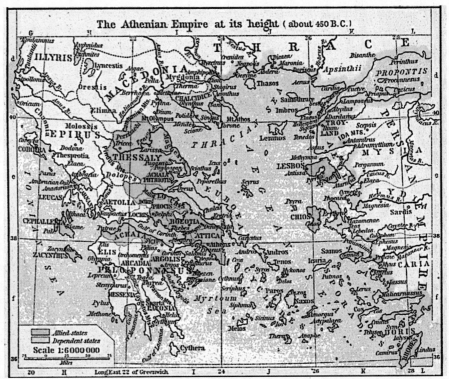

ABOVE: The Delian League, later the Athenian Empire, extended along the Aegean Sea to the shores of Asia Minor. (Public Domain)

men of Athens. For such a leader as Pericles, the public disclosure and proof of Aspasia's direct involvement would have been a terrible blow to his prestige, and political opponents did use this issue to their advantage.

The name of Pericles surfaces in 472 BC as the financier of the production of the Persian Trilogy, written by the famed playwright Aeschylus and in 463 BC during a prosecution of Cimon, a military commander and statesman accused of negligence during a recent military conflict. Cimon was a political rival of Pericles, whose service to Athens in military and diplomatic roles was well known. However, his support of the conservative assembly of the aeropagus often brought friction with the larger ekklesia assembly, to which Pericles and his mentor, Ephialtes, ascribed.

Pericles prosecuted Cimon a second time in 461 BC and succeeded in having his rival ostracized. The practice of ostracism emanated from the ekklesia and provided for the banishment of an individual from Athens for a period of 10 years on the basis of a vote of no fewer than 6,000 Athenian citizens. The voters etched the name of the individual they wanted to ostracize on pottery shards called "ostraka." The ekklesia decided annually whether to hold an ostracism, and when the process was authorized the individual receiving the highest number of votes was sent from the city but retained their Athenian citizenship and ownership of property. Prominent citizens such as Themistocles, hero of the Persian Wars, Alcibiades, a statesman, orator, and military commander, and Thucydides were each ostracized. Pericles' own name appeared on ostraka at times.

In the end, an agreement was reached between Cimon and Pericles that allowed the former to return to Athens, and in fact, Cimon is credited with brokering the peace of 451 BC that paused hostilities between the rival city states.

Pericles extended his power and influence after the assassination of Ephialtes in 461 BC.

ABOVE: Pericles ordered the construction of the Acropolis to begin in the 5th century BC. (No Restrictions via Wikipedia)

He commanded Athenian forces in several battles and won a naval victory over Corinth in 454 BC. The subsequent truce with the Spartans provided an opportunity to focus inward temporarily. Although Periclese's issuance of the Congress Decree, an initiative to unite all of Greece into one nation in 449 BC, came to naught because of Sparta's unwillingness to participate in negotiations, it is evidence of his widening political view.

Despite sporadic internal criticism and uprisings within the Athenian "empire," Pericles led the establishment of Athenian settlements in some areas to strengthen the city state's control and expelled invading barbarians from Thrace in his most celebrated military campaign. The so-called Thirty Years Peace was concluded in 446 BC as Athens gave up control of territory in Boeotia, Euboea, and Megara, choosing to concentrate on a maritime empire, and inducing the Spartan army to withdraw from its doorstep in the Attic peninsula. However, the conflict did erupt once more in 431 BC.

During the interlude before the resumption of the Peloponnesian War and even as it raged once again, Pericles presided over tremendous cultural advances in Athens and fostered an enthusiasm for these achievements, particularly crediting democracy as a facilitator of such benefits, although the assembly regularly bent to the singular will of the "First Citizen of Athens." In his funeral oration, lauding the courage of those lost in battle, the sacrifice of their families, and the common Athenian heritage, he stated, "Our constitution does not copy the laws of neighbouring states; we are rather a pattern to others than imitators ourselves. Its administration favours the many instead of the few; this is why it is called a democracy... The freedom which we enjoy in our government extends also to our ordinary life. There, far from exercising a jealous surveillance over each other, we do not feel called upon to be angry with our neighbour for doing what he likes..."

One of the most remarkable aspects of Pericles' leadership is the soaring cultural

achievement which occurred even during wartime. Construction of the Parthenon began in 447 BC, and other buildings of the Acropolis, such as the temple of Athena Nike and the Propylae, followed. Athens flourished as a centre of the arts. In addition to Aeschylus, the playwrights Sophocles, Euripides, and Aristophanes were active. The renowned sculptor Phidias worked during the period, as did the great philosopher Socrates, and Hippocrates, the famed ancient physician.

During the Age of Pericles, Athens reached the zenith of its glory. Then, the long shadow of war took a vengeful toll. Pericles pursued an unpopular strategy with renewed hostilities, calling the population into Athens itself and requiring the abandonment of homes and farms to the Spartans. He was briefly removed from office and fined, but after reinstatement took no further major action, perishing in the plague that ravaged the crowded streets of Athens along with about one-third of the city's population.

Without the leadership of Pericles, Athens drifted inexorably toward defeat at the hands of the Spartans. Successors paled in comparison to the leadership of the First Man. The mark of Pericles on Western history is indelible, and in it lies something of a paradox. While he led Athens into grinding warfare and sometimes appeared a populist playing to the emotion of the masses, he championed an environment that inspired the thinkers and doers of his day to achievements that resonate with the people even in modern times.

ABOVE: Pericles addresses the people of Athens. He led the city state for three decades, and Thucydides called him the 'First Man' of Athens. (Public Domain)

ABOVE: The Parthenon, an architectural masterpiece, crowns the Acropolis above the ancient city of Athens. (Public Domain)

THE PELOPONNESIAN WAR

The Greek city states had banded together to defeat the invading Persians in the early 5th century BC. However, the spirit of cooperation that had led to the stunning victory faded rapidly after the immediate threat subsided. Of course, the rivalry that had existed among the principal city states, Athens and Sparta, had simmered just below the surface during the fight for survival against the common enemy. Inevitably, the mutual distrust and antipathy of the past emerged with renewed energy in the decades that followed.

During the fight against the Persians, Athens had become a substantial naval power, the greatest of the city states and rivalled only slightly by the Corinthian fleet. The Athenian navy was, in fact, one of the strongest in the Mediterranean world, and it served as a deterrent to invasion by other regional powers and to dissuade marauding pirates from attacking the merchant vessels that plied seaborne trade routes. Meanwhile, the fighting prowess of Sparta had been displayed for the rest of the combatants to observe, and the Spartan ranks were dominant on land.

The leaders of both Sparta and Athens cast about the Greek world in search of allies. Athens assembled the Delian League, founded on the island of Delos, which included more than 300 city states. Prominent among them were Lesbos, Samos, Naxos, Paros, and Aegina, many of the members located in Ionia, a region of modern Turkey. The Spartans led the Peloponnesian League, consisting primarily of Corinth, Thebes, Tegea, Elias, and numerous other city states.

As Athens asserted naval pre-eminence, it achieved great wealth largely at the expense of the other members of the Delian League. A pair of old fortifications called the "Long Walls" were rebuilt as a security measure intended to protect the supply route to the city proper from the port of Piraeus. The Athenians considered the landward threat

ABOVE: Warships of the formidable Athenian navy are shown during the Peloponnesian War. (Public Domain)

ABOVE: Athenian troops under Alcibiades return to Athens after a victory in the Peloponnesian War. (Public Domain)

ABOVE: Athenian leader Nicias brought a peace that was destined to collapse. (Public Domain)

and reasoned that in the event of a siege resupply by sea would be accomplished with the protection of the fleet, while elements of the navy might also raid the enemy's commerce and attack its cities.

The Spartans watched warily as Athenian influence spread across the eastern Mediterranean. They believed the construction of the Long Walls was a provocation, while Athenian domination in the region would be detrimental to trade and should be opposed by any means necessary. While negotiations took place periodically, no real breakthrough seemed likely. Sharp skirmishes broke out from time to time between neighbouring city states, and the two sides probed one another for any sign of military weakness or lack of political resolve.

In 459 BC, the Peloponnesian League was threatened when two of its members,

Corinth and Megara, went to war with one another. Athens stepped in to conclude an alliance with Megara, and the treaty provided the Athenians with a military presence on the isthmus where the city of Corinth was located. The conflict widened and has become known to some historians as the First Peloponnesian War.

In swift retaliation for the Athenian affront, Sparta launched an invasion of the Attic peninsula and threated the city of Athens itself. Startled by the swiftness of the Spartan response, Athens gave up its short-lived territorial gains, and the fighting ceased while the two sides negotiated in early 445 BC. Each grudgingly acknowledged the sphere of influence of the other, and a period known as the Thirty Years' Peace ensued. However, none of the underlying issues that brought on armed conflict in the past really

ABOVE: Athenian and Greek troops clash in battle in Poteidaea. (Public Domain)

subsided during this time, yielding only the outward appearance of true accord.

The years of so-called peace were rather turbulent, particularly among the members of the Delian League as Samos sought to exit the alliance and insurrection followed. While Sparta and Corinth considered the possibility of intervening on the side of Samos, other members of the Peloponnesian League, probably tired of war, declined to do so. Such an intervention would surely have led to a major war between Athens and Sparta just five years after their shaky understanding had been concluded.

Not long after the Samos uprising subsided, the colony of Korkyra revolted against Corinth and appealed to Athens for military aid. The Athenians dispatched a small contingent of naval warships to support the upstart Korkyran fleet. When the Battle of Sybota ended in a draw in 433 BC, the Corinthian plan to carry the fight all the way to Korkyra itself unravelled.

Interestingly, the animosity between Corinth and Athens was the match that set off the proverbial powder keg of the Peloponnesian War that erupted in earnest in 431 BC. The flashpoint of hostilities was Poteidaea, a Corinthian colony with commercial and economic ties to Athens. Thrace, a region to the northeast of Athens and separated from it by the straits of the Bosporus and Dardanelles, was rich in timber and precious minerals. The Athenians demanded that Poteidaea dismantle defences that had been erected along the trade route and allow free access for Athenian commerce with Thrace.

When Poteidaea refused the Athenian demand, Athens concluded a formal alliance with Korkyra and laid siege to Poteidaea. The provocative move was a direct threat to the security of Corinth. Meanwhile, under mounting pressure from Athens, the Poteidaeans sent a plea for military assistance to Sparta.

The Spartans attempted to avoid war, offering to negotiate with the Athenians and find some compromise. Just as Pericles, one of the leaders of Athens, was urging a rejection of the Spartan overture, Thebes, an ally of Sparta, attacked neighbouring Plataea. Coupled with the Theban offensive, the refusal of the Athenians to come to the negotiating table triggered all-out war between the city states.

Spartan King Archidamus II led the army of the Peloponnesian League in an invasion of the Attic peninsula and appealed to Persia, the old enemy of the city states, for assistance in putting an end to the condition he described as a lengthy period of Athenian oppression. The Spartans put many homes and farmsteads to the torch, pillaging and devastating the countryside as they advanced. Pericles responded by avoiding a pitched land battle. He was willing to sacrifice the outlying areas of Athenian influence while Athens itself was secure on the landward side behind the Long Wall defences. Piraeus, the Athenian lifeline to the sea, could be defended in this way while the powerful Athenian navy would dominate the approaches, raid Spartan settlements and outposts, and engage the small Spartan navy in actions that would ultimately prove inconclusive.

Although the tactics that Pericles pursued were effective for a while, the destruction wrought by the Spartan army weighed heavily on the Athenians, as did the necessity of maintaining the fighting efficiency of their soldiers amid close quarters that were essentially siege conditions. While the Spartans had taken

ABOVE: The Athenian army is destroyed at Syracuse during the second failed expedition. (Public Domain)

ABOVE: Spartans under Lysander destroy the walls of Athens in 404 BC. (Public Domain)

ABOVE: Spartan commander Lysander directs his forces outside the walls of Athens. (Public Domain)

a terrible toll in lives and property, a terrible plague swept through the halls and streets of Athens in 429 BC, killing roughly one-third of the city's population, including Pericles.

The Spartans laid siege to Plataea, an Athenian ally, and that city succumbed in 427 BC. Despite its losses, however, Athens held on, its forces repulsing Spartan attacks against outposts west of the city. Spartan efforts to aid forces that had risen against Athens on the island of Lesbos were also turned back.

Remarkably, Athens survived the devastating plague and revived militarily. After choking off the rebellion in Lesbos, the Athenians assumed the offensive and moved westward against the Peloponnesian peninsula itself, landing troops there and attacking Spartan defences. At the same time, the Athenians mounted an unsuccessful expedition across the Mediterranean against the city state of Syracuse in southeastern Sicily.

Both sides were being bled white and losing valuable resources as the war dragged on. Sparta found itself on the brink of capitulation, but peace overtures were initially rejected. Then a reversal of fortune gave the Spartans new life. A significant victory at Chalcidice quelled the thought of defeat, and the hero of the battle, Brasidas, offered them hope. In 422 BC, a great battle was fought at Amphipolis, and the Spartans won another decisive victory.

Both Brasidas and the Athenian commander, a firebrand named Cleon, were killed in the fighting at Amphipolis. With the death of Cleon, his rival, Nicias, was able to persuade the leaders of Athens to accept Sparta's offer of a negotiated end to the war. The subsequent Peace of Nicias was concluded in 421 BC. No major battles were fought during the following six years, but small clashes of arms were frequent while political manoeuvring and intrigue caused tensions to escalate from time to time. Both Sparta and Athens attempted to bring more of the smaller city states into their alliances.

By 415 BC, Athens renewed hostilities with an ill-fated campaign to conquer all of

Sicily. War raged for another 11 years, and the Athenians laid siege to Syracuse for a second time. Although their forces made headway early in the fighting, resistance mounted. The Athenians sustained heavy casualties, particularly when facing strong Syracusan cavalry formations. Sparta entered the war in 413 BC, and the Athenians were then obliged to defend their homeland, compromising their ability to augment the forces engaged in Sicily. Eventually, the Athenian army in Sicily was annihilated. The loss was a staggering blow from which Athens never fully recovered.

Once again, the Spartans invaded the Attic peninsula, laying waste to the countryside as they had done previously. The fortunes of war contributed to political turmoil in Athens, as the democratic government was briefly displaced by a structure known as the "Five Thousand." However, a rapid naval action that was successful just prior to an attack on the city by its own forces restored the Athenian democracy.

The focus of the war shifted toward the sea, where the superior Athenian navy won several decisive victories over the Spartan fleet. Stalemate loomed as neither side could gain a distinct advantage. However, the Spartan hero Lysander won the decisive victory of the Peloponnesian War at the naval Battle of Aegospotami in 405 BC. It was accomplished with aid supplied by the Persians, once their sworn enemy.

The outlook following Aegospotami was bleak for the Athenians. With their naval might shattered, the city of Athens was at the mercy of the Spartans. By the spring of 404 BC, the great city had been starved into submission.

Sparta emerged victorious from the long and costly Peloponnesian War, but the victory was somewhat pyrrhic. The wealth, prestige, military capability, and cultural and political influence of all the city states had waned, particularly that of Athens.

ABOVE: On orders from Lysander Persians assassinate the Athenian commander Alcibiades in exile. (Public Domain)

ABOVE: Widespread suffering is depicted as a plague sweeps through Athens killing one-third of the population. (Public Domain)

KING PHILIP II AND MACEDONIA

North of the Peloponnese, the kingdom of Macedonia had long been influenced by the culture of the Greeks. The Macedonians spoke a dialect of the Greek language, and the ruling family traced its lineage to the bloodline of the gods.

But there were differences. Macedonia was a monarchy, while many of the city states were exercising more participatory forms of government. Further, the city states were more cosmopolitan, while Macedonia was considered the back country, rural, and probably best suited to provide timber and other resources.

Things began to change, however, when Philip II became the Macedonian king in 359 BC at the age of only 23. Born in 382 BC, he was the 18th king of Macedonia and the son of Amyntas, who presided over a chaotic era for the region. As a youth, Philip experienced a tumultuous period in which the kingdom nearly came apart. His father and two brothers were unable to restore order as the strong city state of Thebes intervened regularly in Macedonian affairs and the Illyrians invaded from the northwest.

After the death of Amyntas, the older brothers of Philip, Alexander I and Perdiccas III, ruled for relatively short periods, but both of them died as well, Perdiccus III in battle against the Illyrians. The boy Amyntas IV became king after the demise of Perdiccus III, and Philip became his nephew's regent. Soon enough, though, he took the throne for himself.

King Philip II surveyed the situation. The loyalties of the people were divided, many of them more devoted to clans and chieftains than to the central ruler. The army was in a sad state and needed to be revitalized. The king set to work.

As a boy, Philip had witnessed the combat prowess of the fine Theban army. Held hostage there for a time, he studied their fighting techniques and admired their operational discipline in the field. Philip learned these lessons well and used his understanding of military tactics and training along with his substantial diplomatic skills to win the support of the nobles and chieftains who led the inhabitants of the rugged and mountainous interior of Macedonia. The process was accomplished with remarkable swiftness as Philip forged a national identity in the kingdom and raised an army numbering up to 40,000 highly disciplined and well-trained soldiers.

Just a year after taking the throne, Philip led the Macedonian army into neighbouring Paeonia, where he defeated the Illyrians. He followed with a strategic marriage to Princess Olympias of Epirus, the daughter of King Neoptolemus I, and secured the western borders of his realm. In 356 BC, he conquered the city state of Crenides, using

ABOVE: King Philip II of Macedonia conquered most of Greece and fathered Alexander the Great. (Public Domain)

ABOVE: Macedonian troops defeat the combined forces of Athens, Thebes, and Corinth at the Battle of Chaereonea. (Public Domain)

ABOVE: Olympias, one of the wives of Philip II and mother of Alexander, is shown on this medallion. (Creative Commons Fotogeniss via Wikipedia)

ABOVE: This gold gorgon head decorated the breastplate of the armour belonging to King Philip II.
(Creative Commons Mary Harrsch via Wikipedia)

a threat from the Thracians against it as a pretext for his own occupation. He later succeeded in bringing the Third Sacred War to a close and ending a decade-long conflict with Athens in 346 BC.

Philip's growing power was considered a continuing threat, and six years later Athenian leaders called for action against the Macedonian king. Their declaration was a violation of the terms they had concluded with the Macedonians, and Philip sent his army southward in a war of conquest. At the Battle of Chaeronea in 338 BC, the Macedonians defeated the Greek Confederation, principally the allied forces of Athens, Corinth, and Thebes. After that pivotal victory, Philip was master of the major Greek city states with the exception of Sparta.

Through diplomatic pressure and persuasion, bribery, and coercion, Philip succeeded in cobbling together a coalition of city states called the Corinthian League. Rather than fighting among themselves, he expected the convention to become a deterrent to the

continuing aggression of Greece's perennial enemy, Persia. The Corinthian League was formed in 337 BC, and a year later, the king announced a punitive expedition against the Persians. He explained that his motivation was retribution against Persia for the many years of suffering the enemy had inflicted on the city states of Greece.

While Philip was busy conquering most of Greece, he married seven times. These unions were generally in the hopes of solidifying new alliances or meant as gestures of goodwill. The most important of these marriages was to Olympias of Epirus. She was the mother of Alexander, the future warrior king who would gain lasting fame. A daughter, Cleopatra, was also born to Philip and Olympias.

When Alexander was born, Philip was with his army and completing the capture of Potidea. The historian Plutarch wrote, "Just after Philip had taken Potidea, he received three messages at one time, that Parmenio had overthrown the Illyrians in a great battle, that his race horse had won the course at the Olympic games, and that his wife had given birth to Alexander…"

Issues arose as Alexander matured. His mother was from Epirus, a neighbouring region, while advisors petitioned Philip to marry a Macedonian woman and produce an heir with pure Macedonian blood. Alexander was enraged when Attalus, a Macedonian military commander, convinced Philip to marry his niece, Cleopatra Eurydice. Accounts vary as to the series of events that followed. However, both Alexander and Olympias either left Philip's court on their own or were temporarily exiled because of an outburst by Alexander during the wedding of Cleopatra Eurydice and Philip in response to an outrageous declaration from Attalus. According to Plutarch, Attalus "in his drink desired the Macedonians would implore the gods to give them a lawful successor to the kingdom by his niece."

ABOVE: Pausanius assassinates King Philip II during the festivities surrounding his daughter's wedding.
(Public Domain)

Just before the Macedonian military expedition was due to march against Persia, Philip's daughter, Cleopatra, was to be married to Alexander of Epirus, the brother of Olympias. During the merriment and feasting that followed, an assassin named Pausanias killed Philip, either by stabbing him or drawing his bow and shooting an arrow through the king's eye. The killer's motivation was apparently some grievance against both Philip and Attalus.

Again, accounts vary, some relating that Philip never intended to sire an heir to displace Alexander and the two were reconciled, while others assert that Olympias and Alexander were under suspicion for prompting the assassin to act. Years later, Aristotle, who had been Alexander's teacher, wrote that he did not believe there had been a conspiracy and that Philip had been killed solely due to the motives of Pausanias.

The end of King Philip II was ignominious, and the likely outcome of his pending military expedition against Persia is the subject of debate. However, what is clearly known is that his military victories that led to dominance over much of Greece facilitated the rise of his son Alexander to the throne of Macedonia at the age of 21 in 336 BC.

Philip's military lieutenants perhaps believed that they could control the young monarch. However, Alexander was soon to display remarkable competence and determination to continue his father's military opposition to Persia. In fact, the young ruler's ambitions were to extend the dominion of Greece to its absolute limit during his lifetime.

ABOVE: The tomb of King Philip II of Macedonia is located in Vergina in northeastern Greece. (Public Domain)

ALEXANDER THE GREAT

In the pantheon of the world's great conquerors, there is no name more synonymous with military victory, strategic and tactical prowess, and diplomatic ability. The mere mention of his name conjures images of martial shock and awe. For 11 years, the young king of Macedonia campaigned and conquered much of the known world. And in his wake came the Hellenization of Eastern lands, as well as the seeds of empire that brought far-reaching consequences to Western civilization, the reverberations of which are still felt across nearly two and one-half millennia.

The son of King Philip II, Alexander the Great was born in 356 BC in the city of Pella in central Macedonia. His mother was Olympias, daughter of King Neoptolemus of Epira. He came to the throne of Macedonia upon the assassination of his father under circumstances that are still unclear and after a family rift over the possibility of his accession had led to separation and reconciliation with his father.

As a boy, Alexander was taught the skills of the horseman and warrior by Leonidas, a relative of his mother. He became hardened to the rigors of the field and grew into a young man of physical strength, stamina, and iron will. Intellectually, from the age of 12 until 16 he was taught by Aristotle, one of the renowned thinkers and intellectuals of the day. From an early age, Olympias encouraged his personal belief that he had descended from the gods themselves, and considering his accomplishments there were some who did not doubt that assertion.

THE MACEDONIAN PHALANX—BATTLE OF THE CARTS
ABOVE: The Macedonian phalanx is used to deadly effect in battle with the Thracians. (Public Domain)

ABOVE: In this 18th century painting, Alexander cuts through the Gordian Knot with his sword. (Public Domain)

ABOVE: This iconic mosaic of Alexander the Great was found in a house in the Roman city of Pompeii. (Public Domain)

When Alexander was only 16, in 340 BC, Philip set out to campaign in Byzantium, leaving the boy responsible for Macedonia. In the absence of the king, Alexander defeated the Maedi, a Thracian people. Two years later, he commanded the left flank of Philip's army in the defeat of the allied Greek city states at Chaeronea. Upon Philip's death, Alexander's reign was endorsed by the army, and he solidified his position, ordering the execution of all rivals for the throne and the princes of Lycenstis, a province of upper Macedonia, who were implicated in a possible assassination plot against the late king. Conjecture still surrounds the possibility that Alexander and Olympias had conspired to murder Philip, who was either stabbed to death or shot through the eye with an arrow by a disgruntled ex-lover named Pausanias during the wedding celebration of Philip's daughter, Cleopatra.

At the time of his death, Philip had prepared a military campaign against the Persian Empire and King Darius III. The Persian domain stretched from the Balkans to the frontier of present-day India, and Philip's burning desire to conquer in the East was

ABOVE: In this 1665 painting, Alexander leads his army to victory at the Battle of Granicus. (Public Domain)

ABOVE: In a drunken rage, Alexander kills his friend Cleitus. He immediately regretted the terrible act. (Public Domain)

passed to an ambitious Alexander. First, he campaigned in Thrace and the Balkans, and in 335 BC, he vanquished Thebes, a rebellious Greek city state, razing the city, slaughtering many, and selling others into bondage.

Alexander then turned his gaze toward Persia, where he intended to free the cities of Greek heritage in Asia Minor and along the Mediterranean coast, take the wealth of the historical enemy of Greece, and even venture beyond. He is said to have visited the site of ancient Troy and in 334 BC defeated the Persian army and its large complement of Greek mercenaries at the Battle of Granicus in western Turkey.

According to Arrian, a historian of the Roman period, much of the 40,000-man

Persian army was destroyed, while the cities of the region fell into Alexander's hands. Alexander released his fleet and refused to do battle at sea, effectively neutralizing the Persian navy by taking each of its port cities from the landward.

Within a year, Alexander supposedly reached Gordium in Phrygia, where the legend of the Gordian Knot arises. The story goes that the complicate knot was tied to an oxcart and the man who untied it was destined to rule all of Asia. Alexander took up the challenge, but instead of fumbling with the knot, he severed it with a blow of his sword. Whether the story is apocryphal or there is some shred of truth in it, such is the making of a man who grew larger than life.

The Battle of Issus, fought in 333 BC in southern Turkey near the border with

modern Syria, was pivotal in Alexander's campaign of conquest. When Alexander did not immediately come out to battle Darius III on an open plain, the Persian king interpreted the hesitation as a sign of weakness. Instead, Alexander lured his enemy into a chase, which concluded in a narrow space where the advantage of Persian numbers was neutralized. The Macedonian army won a great victory, and Darius fled the field, leaving his immediate family behind. When the mother, wife, two daughters, and infant son of Darius were brought to Alexander, he ordered them treated with courtesy and respect.

Arrian wrote that when Darius proposed a ransom payment for the release of his family, Alexander responded curtly, "In the future, whenever you send word to me, address me as

ABOVE: Alexander raises his sword at Granicus. His friend Cleitus saved his life during the melee. (Public Domain)

ABOVE: Alexander and his army defeat the forces of Persian King Darius III at the pivotal Battle of Gaugamela. (Public Domain)

ABOVE: In this 1602 painting Jan Brueghel the Elder created a panoramic view of the deadly swirl of combat at Gaugamela. (Public Domain)

the king of Asia and not as an equal, and let me know, as the master of all that belonged to you, if you have need of anything."

Moving southward along the Mediterranean coast, Alexander subdued numerous cities, denying the Persian fleet a safe harbour. He laid siege to the city of Tyre, which fell after seven long months. It was perhaps his greatest military victory. In the midst of the siege, Darius made a new offer. He would cede all his lands west of the River Euphrates and pay 10,000 talents in gold for the release of his family. Alexander's advisor, Parmenion, who had also served his father, offered, "I would accept, were I Alexander." The conqueror retorted, "I too, were I Parmenion."

Continuing southward, Alexander subjugated Egypt and received the crown of Pharaoh. He founded the city of Alexandria, one of several that would bear his name, along the Mediterranean coast near the western course of the River Nile and became thoroughly engrossed in its planning. Arrian reported, "A sudden passion for the project

seized him, and he himself marked out where the agora was to be built and decided how many temples were to be erected and to which gods they were to be dedicated."

Alexander consulted the fabled Oracle of Amon, receiving the greeting of a pharaoh. He did not reveal the oracle's message and returned to Tyre in the spring of 331 BC before crossing into Mesopotamia toward the River Tigris. Darius marched to meet the Macedonian army, and the two forces clashed in the epic Battle at Gaugamela in northern Iraq on October 31. Control of the eastern half of the Persian Empire was at stake.

Arrian described the battle. "For a brief period the fighting was hand to hand, but when Alexander and his horsemen pressed the enemy hard, shoving the Persians and striking their faces with spears, and the Macedonian phalanx, tightly arrayed and bristling with pikes, was already upon them, Darius, who had long been in a state of dread, now saw terrors all around him; he wheeled about – the first to do so – and fled."

Alexander prevailed, and his army pursued the defeated Persians for 35 miles.

The conqueror entered the city of Babylon, and the Persian capital at Susa also fell, yielding 50,000 gold talents. Vesting the Persian satrap, or regional governor, with responsibility for the continuing administrative function of the area, Alexander demonstrated a willingness to incorporate the conquered into the framework of his own society without foisting Macedonian custom upon them. He also placed the newly won treasure in the keeping of a Persian trustee. He left Darius's family in comfort at Susa, and Parmenion remained in Media.

Alexander moved on to Persepolis, where he burned the palace of King Xerxes to the ground in retribution for his campaign against Greece in 480 BC. About this time, Darius was murdered by his own troops at the urging of Bessus, one of his satraps. The death of Darius was the last remaining obstacle to Alexander's claim as "King of the East" or "Lord of Asia." Wishing to foster a peaceful revision of rule

ABOVE: Persian King Darius III lost his empire to the invading Macedonian army under Alexander the Great. (Creative Commons Carole Raddato via Wikipedia)

ABOVE: This tapestry depicting Alexander at Gaugamela by Charles Le Brun was presented at the court of his patron, French King Louis XIV. (Creative Commons via Wikipedia)

ABOVE: In the Battle of the Hydaspes, the Macedonian phalanx fights the elephants of Porus. (Public Domain)

in the East, Alexander honoured Darius with a royal burial. He understood that political control was more easily achieved through respect for the culture of the conquered. His commitment was evidenced by his personal adoption of certain Persian customs and his donning of Persian dress.

For three years, Alexander continued to campaign into Central Asia, crossing the Elburz Mountains to the shore of the Caspian Sea, seizing cities and defeating the tribal armies that opposed him. The Greek mercenaries who had followed Darius finally surrendered to him. In the region of Aria, he accepted the submission of the Satibarzanes only to crush them when they proved turncoats and revolted.

Despite his success, Alexander remained wary of his old comrade and his father's trusted lieutenant, Parmenion. An opportunity to eliminate the perceived threat materialized when Parmenion's son, Philotas, the commander of an elite cavalry formation, was accused of plotting to assassinate Alexander or at least with failing to report his knowledge of a plot. The accusation was upheld by the army, and the son was duly executed. Alexander then moved against the father and the rest of the family. He sent a secret message to Cleander, Parmenion's second in command, instructing him to eliminate Parmenion.

Cleander carried out the order, and though there was some shock in the wake of Alexander's ruthlessness, the leader's position was strengthened. This was particularly true as all of Parmenion's close associates were

murdered. Then Cleitus and Hephaestion, two trusted military men, took control of the reorganized cavalry, the superb shock troops and elite warriors of Alexander's army. As the winter of 329 BC approached, the Macedonian army advanced to the site of modern Kabul, capital of Afghanistan.

Bessus, the treacherous betrayer of Darius, was known to be forming an army in Bactria, an ancient region of Iran. Alexander crossed the high mountains of the Hindu Kush, west of the Himalayas. His men endured the arduous march, experiencing food and water shortages, but pushing Bessus westward. As he passed through the country, Alexander appointed native satraps to administer the newly acquired lands. Crossing the River Oxus, called the Amu Darya today, he sent his lieutenant Ptolemy to chase down and subdue Bessus. When Bessus was captured, he was flogged and turned over to the Persians, who brutally meted out their own brand of

ABOVE: In the heat of an argument, Alexander kills his friend Cleitus in this painting by Daniel de Blieck. (Public Domain)

ABOVE: Alexander the Great shows mercy to the family of the Persian King Darius III after their capture. (Public Domain)

justice, cutting off his ears and nose. Bessus was put to death soon afterward.

Alexander's desire for military campaigning remained insatiable, and he advanced to the frontier of modern Pakistan, establishing another of the cities he dubbed "Alexandria." A tribal uprising was defeated over several difficult months, following up that victory with the defeat of holdouts under the leader Oxyartes. When Oxyartes capitulated, among the captives was his daughter, Roxana. In a gesture of goodwill, Alexander married the girl. His diplomatic overture secured the loyalty of some, while those who remained adamantly opposed to the new order were decimated in combat.

The army came to rest at Maracanda in modern Uzbekistan, and Alexander committed a reprehensible act during a

ABOVE: Alexander the Great's forces assault the city walls during the siege of Tyre. (Public Domain)

ABOVE: Bucephalus rears as Alexander attempts to calm the great horse in this painting by Domenico Maria Canuti. (Public Domain)

drunken argument with Cleitus, his close friend who had saved his life on the battlefield at Granicus. The violent disagreement, fuelled by the consumption of copious amounts of wine, erupted when Cleitus objected to Alexander's conspicuous adoption of Persian dress and customs. Cleitus admonished Alexander to maintain respect for Macedonian tradition and raised his right hand to has commander's face stating, "This is the hand, Alexander, that saved you then."

Enraged, Alexander impaled Cleitus with a spear. Afterward, Alexander expressed sincere remorse, but the army dutifully passed a resolution that posthumously accused Cleitus of treason. Still, according to Arrian,

Alexander was distraught. "Again, and again, he called himself his friend's murderer and went without food and drink for three days and completely neglected his person."

Despite his regret, Alexander may well have already been gravitating toward a despotic perspective on his rule. He began earnestly to consider his own deification. Still, his military ambition was unbridled. He crossed the Hindu Kush once again and divided his army, sending a contingent through the Khyber Pass and leading the remainder on a northerly route through rugged country. High on a mountaintop, the fortress of Aornos was taken by storm in a magnificent feat of arms, and in the spring of 326 BC, the reunited army crossed the River Indus, where he made alliances with Taxiles and Porus, two leaders previously at war

ABOVE: Alexander the Great grasps the bridle of Bucephalus while wearing full armour. (Public Domain)

with one another. His army had defeated Porus at the Battle of the the Hydaspes in Punjab, a region of modern India and Pakistan.

Alexander founded two more cities at that time, another Alexandria and the second named Bucephala, in memory of his famous horse, Bucephalus, who died after being wounded in the Battle of the Hydaspes. Bucephalus remains one of the most famous war horses of ancient history. He was said to be of "the best Thessalian strain," a massive horse with a star on his forehead. Legend says that the horse was offered for sale to King Philip II for the high price of 13 talents. Philip turned away because the horse was wild and no one could tame it.

Alexander spoke up, saying that he would pay the purchase price if he failed to bring Bucephalus under control. The young man approached the horse, turned him away from the sun so that his shadow was not visible, and whispered softly to the animal. Within minutes, the partnership was complete, and those who saw what Alexander accomplished were thoroughly impressed. When Bucephalus died, Alexander's grief was readily apparent.

The victory at the Hydaspes was Alexander's last great battle. He marched on to Hyphasis and may have had designs on reaching the River Ganges. Although he wished to press forward, his weary army mutinied at the prospect. After Coenus, a senior commander, addressed Alexander on their behalf, he agreed to turn and march for home. Prior to departing Hyphasis, Alexander build 12 altars honouring the 12 gods who resided on Mount Olympus. Moving by land and water, the army fought continually, and Alexander was seriously wounded.

The army was divided, some moving by water and others by land through Quetta and Kandahar into the Helmand Valley. On the landward route, a barren desert was devoid of water, and many died, including women and children. Once the army had been reunited, Alexander continued a policy of pacifying the conquered lands, appointing satraps he believed he could trust while removing and executing

ABOVE: This bust of Alexander the Great dates to the Hellenistic period, either the 1st or 2nd century BC.
(Public Domain)

those who had committed financial crimes or failed to carry out their duties. Alexander was pitiless in his exertion of authority.

After returning to Susa in the spring of 324 BC, Alexander and dozens of his officers took Persian wives. He hoped that these unions would advance his agenda of bringing the Hellenistic and Persian cultures together. However, there was relatively little enthusiasm for such a fusion among the Macedonians. A second mutiny occurred that year at Opis, but swift reconciliation followed.

In the autumn of 324 BC, Hephaestion died suddenly of a fever, and Alexander mourned profusely. He spared no expense, and the royal funeral in Babylon included a pyre that cost 10,000 talents. Afterward, Alexander's behaviour deteriorated. He drank heavily, and his paranoia increased. He contemplated his own deification again, and most of the cities under his rule complied. Spartans derided the claim, though. Their

famous declaration read, "Since Alexander wishes to be a god, let him be a god."

By the winter of 324 BC, Alexander was at the head of a punitive expedition against Luristan in northern Iran. He dispatched another force to explore the upper reaches of the Caspian Sea and planned to improve communications between Babylon and the regions eastward. He is believed to have been preparing for a military expedition into the Arabian peninsula while engaged in an engineering project to bring irrigation to areas surrounding the River Euphrates and considering an effort to colonize the coastline of the Persian Gulf.

He fell ill after an overindulgence of food and drink during a lengthy banquet and died after 10 days of fever and delirium in June of 323 BC. His reign concluded after 12 years and eight months, while his epic military campaigns had covered a span of 11 years. At the time of his death, Roxana, probably jealous of the Persian wives Alexander had taken, was carrying his unborn son.

Alexander died with no heir and left no specific succession plan. In the immediate aftermath of his death, his generals are said to have temporarily endorsed Philip Arrhidaeus, the mentally slow and illegitimate son of Philip II, or Alexander's unborn son, Alexander IV. They also bargained with one another to govern regions of the far-flung empire. However, both the potential rulers were killed, and years of warfare followed as the lieutenants and their offspring fought for control of the lands stretching from the Mediterranean to the frontier of India.

The long shadow of Alexander the Great remains today. As an innovative military commander, he developed a tremendous cult of personality. He was a shrewd, flexible diplomat, and at times a magnanimous conqueror. He was also ruthless, vain, and boisterous. His influence led to the spread of Greek culture across the known world, ushering in the Hellenistic Period, and it is no exaggeration to assert that he inspired great military and political leaders of the future.

ABOVE: This 19th century engraving conveys the grandeur of Alexander's funeral carriage. (Public Domain)

THE DEATH OF ALEXANDER

In slightly more than a decade of military campaigning, Alexander the Great had conquered much of the known world. By 323 BC, he appeared at the height of his power, and planning and aspirations for further conquest would probably have been in full swing. However, aged only in his 30s, the great Macedonian leader of the Greek army that had conquered lands from the eastern Mediterranean Basin to the valley of the River Indus lay on his deathbed.

Considering the lasting fame Alexander achieved, the fact that his actual cause of death, the location of his death, and the final whereabouts of his tomb remain shrouded in theory and conjecture is somewhat astonishing. According to one source, Alexander died in Babylonia at the court of King Nebuchadnezzar II at the age of 32 on June 10 or 11 of 323 BC. That particular source is Babylonian, and there is little evidence that would corroborate it.

Theories as to the cause of death run the gamut from assassination by strychnine or arsenic or some other form of poisoning, typhoid fever, malaria, liver failure due to alcoholism, or the rampaging infection from wounds received in battle in India. He is thought to have experienced severe abdominal pain that made him cry out in agony, delirium, fever, heavy sweats, and chills during his last days. Those who might have been under suspicion as potential assassins included one of his wives, any of his ambitious subordinate generals including his illegitimate half-brother Ptolemy I Soter, who in fact became one of the future rulers of the divided empire, and perhaps his own trusted cup bearer. Some reports that Alexander became deathly ill after consuming a large bowl of wine might, in

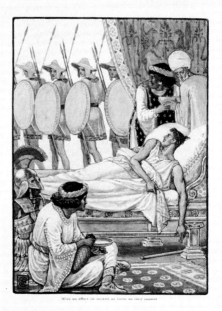

ABOVE: Alexander the Great lies on his deathbed in the year 323 BC after conquering most of the known world. (Public Domain)

fact, indicate that he died of poisoning, but there is little further evidence to support the contention that he was murdered.

Regardless, the great conqueror was to be as influential in world affairs in death as he had been in life. He designated no single heir to his powerful position, and with its strong leader dead the empire might rapidly decline, fading into history almost as quickly as it had risen to prominence.

As Alexander's life ebbed away, his generals gathered around his bed and bent close to their leader. In unison, they asked the question as to which of them should inherit the leading role in the future of the empire. Perhaps not completely coherent,

ABOVE: This poignant sculpture, copied from an original of the 2nd century BC, is titled 'Dying Alexander.' (Creative Commons Urek Meniashvili via Wikipedia)

Alexander is said to have whispered his response: "The fittest."

In the aftermath of Alexander's demise, came the Hellenistic period of ancient Greek history, and while art and culture continued to flourish, the political rivalries and aspirations of his principal lieutenants resulted in the division of the empire that inevitably led to weakness. Alexander's death is a watershed moment in the history of the Western world. This was not only due to his legacy of military achievement and territorial conquest at a tender, youthful age and the aura of invincibility that surrounds the mere mention of his name to this day, but also because it precipitated those rivalries and the empire's vulnerability.

Accounts of the disposition of Alexander's remains are just as inconclusive as the other circumstances surrounding his early death. A funerary cart was supposedly prepared to transport the body from Babylon to Macedonian, and that preparation may have taken as long as two years. Ptolemy I Soter met the cart in Syria and diverted it to Egypt, where it was interred in Memphis. Some years later, it was supposedly removed to Alexandria and reinterred, visited by Caesar Augustus, and its location then somehow lost to history.

ABOVE: The loyal and the ambitious gather at the bedside of the dying Alexander the Great in 323 BC. (Public Domain)

THE HELLENISTIC PERIOD

Generally dating from the death of Alexander the Great in 323 BC to the Battle of Actium and the ascendancy of Caesar Augustus to power in Rome in 31 BC, the Hellenistic period was the last era of independent Greek government and civilization in ancient times. Although ancient Greece had always been a loose collection of fiercely independent city states prone to fighting among themselves as much as with outsiders, ancient Greece was also the cradle of Western culture, thought, and custom. Greek influence stretched from the Mediterranean to the Asian continent and with it came a pronounced political presence and further colonization by the Greek peoples.

Despite its fractious division into separate domains under the generals who sought power for themselves after Alexander's demise, Greek culture continued to flourish during the Hellenistic period. Art and architecture were reflective of emotional connections to dramatic detail and finely crafted, ornate creations. Elaborate temples were built during the period and reflected heretofore inconceivable beauty, size and scope. Greek influence had proliferated across the known world during Alexander's military campaigns, and just as the influence of the conquerors interacted

ABOVE: This gold ceremonial bowl was fashioned by a Greek craftsman during the Hellenistic period.
(Creative Commons Dosseman via Wikipedia)

with the conquered, so too, the cultures of the conquered wrought their influence on the Greeks, whose thirst for knowledge, contemplation of the world around them, and natural curiosity had never waned.

As one observer stated, "Where earlier artists sought to codify a generalized artistic ideal, Hellenistic artists shifted focus to the individual and the specific. They turned increasingly away from the heroic to the everyday, from gods to mortals, from aloof serenity to individual emotion, and from decorous drama to emotional melodrama. Their works appeal to the senses through luscious or lustrous surface treatments and to our hearts as well as our intellects through expressive subjects and poses."

The newly cosmopolitan world of the Greeks introduced a territorial expansion that made individuals more mobile, prone to travel and relocate, and to explore the strange and puzzling customs of other cultures. Diversity brought a desire to seek individual sense of purpose and renewal of personal aspirations. Philosophers such as Epicurus and Diogenes of Sinope became known for

BOVE: The Egyptian god Horus became well known to e Greeks during the Hellenistic period. (Public Domain)

ABOVE: The Hellenistic period produced the magnificent Nike or Winged Victory of Samothrace. (Public Domain)

ABOVE: This Chinese tapestry depicts a tribal warrior beneath an image of a centaur, evidence of Greek influence. (Public Domain)

their views. The former encouraged people to seek happy, tranquil lives and to use philosophy as a tool. He offered that people should spend their lives as self-sufficient as possible and among friends. He concluded that death was the end of the body and soul and that the root of human frailty is the denial of the inevitable. Death, he said, was not to be feared. The gods did exist; however, they played no part in human existence.

"Death does not concern us," commented Epicurus, "because as long as we exist, death is not here. And when it does come, we no longer exist."

The latter was one of the founders of the school of Cynicism. Diogenes of Sinope suggested that the purpose of life was to live virtuously and in harmony with nature, a state that could be realized with the rejection of worldly concerns such as wealth and comfort. The pursuit of such a situation, he said, required rigorous training and thorough commitment.

He commented, "I am Diogenes the dog. I nuzzle the kind, bark at the greedy, and bite scoundrels."

As a result of the Greek territorial expansion over a period of nearly 300 years, the deities of other lands became objects of exploration. The religious practices and the mystical ways of the Near and Middle East,

India, and Egypt gained popularity as Greeks explored the mysticism and cult formation of previously unknown practices. At times, these religious concepts offered an afterlife that was better than the worldly existence, while a wave of ruler worship also emerged. The deification of rulers was especially noteworthy in Ptolemaic Egypt, ruled by a dynasty founded by one of Alexander's generals.

Belgian-born American chemist and historian George Sarton noted, "The Hellenistic world was international to a degree, polyglot and inspired by many religious faiths...the Greek ideals were pagan and the Hellenistic age witnessed their death struggle against Asiatic and Egyptian mysteries, on the one side, and against Judaism, on the other."

The politics of the Hellenistic period were marked by the rivalries among the generals who succeeded Alexander and divided his former empire into separate domains to be ruled individually and by successors. The division inherently weakened Greece, creating opportunities for other civilizations to encroach on Greek territory, incite rebellions, and generally create unrest. Rome was at the height of its expansion during the Hellenistic period, and inevitably its eastern gaze would become more focused following it defeat of rival Carthage in the west and the expansion in Italy and Sicily that took place. In time, the Roman dominion would extend from the Iberian peninsula to Syria in the Middle East, from the British Isles to the shores of Egypt and northward into the heart of Europe.

During the Hellenistic period, the concept of the city state began to fade away, replaced by more centralized government and the power of an individual authority. The glory of the city states of old eroded, and the participatory form of government was

eclipsed in the process. Soon enough, the colossal power of Rome would exert itself.

During the Hellenistic period, Rome conquered the Greek city states of Syracuse and Paestrum on the island of Sicily as well as those of southern Italy. Moving militarily, Roman military expeditions looted the city of Corinth in 146 BC, and Athens was taken by siege in 86 BC. The Romans became enamoured of Greek culture, and rather than crushing it embraced it thoroughly. There were those statesmen who warned Romans against too much assimilation of Greek culture; however, the ways of the Greeks became thoroughly ingrained in Roman civilization, even to the extent that their pantheon of gods was adopted.

The Romans admired Greek art and sculpture and were quite willing to copy what they saw. Many Greek philosophers and teachers were brought to Rome to tutor young men, while others, including Augustus Caesar, travelled to Greece to learn of the arts, sciences, and philosophy. The Roman poet Horace captured the essence of the Greco-Roman experience in his famous commentary, "Captive Greece captured its uncivilized conqueror and brought the arts to rustic Latium."

For many years, the Hellenistic period was probably mischaracterized by some historians who viewed it as simply the bridge between Classical Greece and the imperial age of the Roman Empire. In truth, the limits of human thought, expression, and discovery continued to expand during the period. The great library at Alexandria was founded, while titans of science, mathematics, poetry, and philosophy lived and produced monumental contributions to Western civilization during the period. Among them were Aristotle, Euclid, Archimedes, Eratosthenes, Polybius, and others.

ABOVE: Hellenistic influence is seen in this magnificent sculpture of Buddha. (Public Domain)

ABOVE: Epicurus was a great Greek philosopher of the Hellenistic period. (Public Domain)

THE TWILIGHT OF ANCIENT GREECE

The untimely death of Alexander the Great left a power vacuum that led to years of armed conflict and unrest. He had not named an heir or successor to the throne of his vast empire, and decades of intermittent wars, assassinations, treaties, and alliances made and broken, ensued. From 322 BC until 281 BC, four major wars for empire occurred. Essentially, those generals who had crowded around Alexander's deathbed fought one another to expand their territories and influence. An attempt to divide the empire among numerous former lieutenants at a conference in Babylon had failed to provide a lasting settlement.

The warring generals were referred to as the Diadochi, which translates from the Greek as "successors." With the four wars of the Diadochi, the Hellenistic period emerged. As Alexander conquered, he had brought with him Greek heritage and culture, Hellenizing the subjugated regions. Despite the chaos and uncertainty of the years after Alexander's death, this Hellenizing process continued, diffusing Greek custom and culture across the known world.

Among the youngest senior commanders in Alexander's army, Ptolemy I Soter consolidated power in Egypt by 305 BC and established his capital at Alexandria. Arguably, Ptolemaic Egypt became the most successful of the successor states spawned by Alexander's conquests. While intermittent disagreements occurred elsewhere, Ptolemy

ABOVE: A queen of Ptolemaic Egypt is depicted in this Hellenistic mosaic. (Public Domain)

ABOVE: Cleopatra VII, the ill-fated Ptolemaic queen of Egypt is shown with Julius Caesar in this painting. (Public Domain)

I sought to promote a society that embraced ethnic diversity and a blend of the great cultures of Greece and Egypt. The heart of the realm was the fertile delta of the River Nile, and cultivation of the rich farmland produced substantial harvests that brought trade and commerce to the region, along with substantial wealth.

While Ptolemaic Greece and neighbouring Rhodes gained total control of exports of grain and wine into the region of the Black Sea, seafarers learned the seasonal changes of the weather, winds, and seas, facilitating a brisk trade with the dominions of Arabia and the subcontinent of India. Alexandria surpassed Athens as the preeminent city of Greece, and by the time of the Roman conquest of Greece in the 1st and 2nd centuries BC, its population had exploded to roughly a million people.

Meanwhile, Ptolemy encouraged the sharing of ideas and led the establishment of a state religion that centred on the blending of Osiris, the Egyptian god of the underworld, Apis, the most prevalent of three Egyptian bull cults, and Zeus, the king of the Greek deities, into the god Serapis.

Ptolemy ordered the building of the great lighthouse at Alexandria, which became one of the seven wonders of the ancient world, and the temple of Serapeum was constructed with the fabled Library of Alexandria nearby. Subsequently, Alexandria became a great centre of religion, government, and learning that did indeed rival Athens.

During the 3rd century BC, Ptolemaic Greece had emerged as a Mediterranean naval power, but continuing disputes with the neighbouring Seleucids drained economic and other resources from the dominion, particularly under the rule of successors to Ptolemy I. The kingdom thrived for an extended period, fell into decline approximately 150 years after it was founded, and lingered for more than another century until the death of Cleopatra VII, consort of the Roman leader Marc Antony, in 30 BC.

One of the generals who campaigned with Alexander the Great from the Mediterranean to the frontier of India, Seleucus I Nicator established a domain known to history as Seleucid Greece in 303 BC. The territory included lands in Syria, the Middle East, Mesopotamia, and Asia Minor. Its capital was established at Antioch in present-day Turkey. The Seleucids colonized other regions of the Mediterranean, and their cities were favoured locations for artisans who produced exquisite pottery, perfumes,

ABOVE: Ptolemy I Soter is depicted in this sculpture as the pharaoh of Egypt. (Creative Commons Einsamer Schütze via Wikipedia)

ABOVE: A Seleucid princess marries a monarch from the East to seal a pact of friendship. (Public Domain)

jewellery, woven tapestries and cloth noted for the rich purple hue of its dye.

Heavily engaged in the export of Hellenistic culture, the Seleucids ventured into areas with an incredible diversity of peoples, including Jewish, Phoenician, Persian, and other ethnicities. That diversity, however, along with disputes among competing dynastic rulers, was responsible at least in part for the unrest that continually surfaced across the Seleucid empire for more than a century. While the Seleucids came into conflict with Ptolemaic Greece in the west, to the east there were intermittent clashes with the rulers of the Indian subcontinent.

Seleucid control of Anatolia, the region bounded on the north by the Black Sea, west by the Mediterranean, and to the south and east by the Taurus Mountains, projected tremendous influence across the Middle East, while control of the

ABOVE: Seleucus I Nicator was a trusted lieutenant of Alexander the Great who became a Hellenistic ruler.
(Creative Commons via Wikipedia)

Hellespont (modern Dardanelles) brought a dominant position in trade and commerce through the Black Sea and into the eastern Mediterranean Basin.

However, as early as the 3rd century BC, the Seleucid grip on its territorial holdings had begun to erode. During the next 150 years, cities in the eastern Mediterranean had won their independence from Seleucid domination, and by the death of Antiochus IV in 163 BC, considerable territory in Anatolia had been lost to Roman incursions. One of the vexing phenomena that contributed to the unrest in the Seleucid empire was its effort to Hellenize foreign peoples. The building of a temple to Zeus in Jerusalem during the reign of Antiochus IV in the mid-2nd century BC, for example, along with decrees that restricted Jewish religious practices, sparked the revolt of the Maccabees, which ended with the creation of an autonomous Judea. The Romans completed their conquest of Seleucid Greece in the 1st century BC.

The grandson of Antigonus I Monophthalmus, one of Alexander's most trusted lieutenants and an early successor to his empire, Antigonus Gonatas came to power in Macedonia in 279 BC. Under his rule, Macedonia may have been perceived as less than progressive while Ptolemaic and Seleucid Greece were actively Hellenizing the known world. However, the fact that Macedonia was somewhat isolated in mountainous northern Greece contributed to its reliance on the exploitation of natural resources such as timber and silver to develop robust trade and become quite prosperous.

Macedonia maintained its foremost position among the Greek military powers, and Antigonus invaded Laconia. Later campaigns were undertaken with the aggressive leadership of King Philip V, who led expeditions into the Peloponnese, Ionia,

ABOVE: This Hellenistic statue is believed to be a depiction of a Seleucid prince. (Public Domain)

and the wealthy city of Pergamum in Asia Minor over a 40-year period from 220 BC to 180 BC. Three times during the 2nd century BC, the Macedonians took up arms against the encroaching Roman military machine, even forming an alliance with the Carthaginians under Hannibal during the Second Punic War. Eventually, Macedonia became a Roman province.

Lysimachus, another close associate and successor to Alexander the Great, was killed in battle against the Seleucids at Corupedium, the last battle of the Wars of the Diadochi, in 281 BC. However, about the same time, his dominion in Asia Minor had become somewhat fractious. Philestairos, secretary to Lysimachus, had rebelled against his master and taken control of the city of Pergamum along with much of Lysimachus's treasury. Philestairos later organized troops and helped to fund a military campaign that repulsed an invasion of Anatolia by the Gauls in 270 BC. He earned praise and loyalty from numerous Greek cities along the coast of Anatolia.

Philestairos died in 263 BC and was succeeded by his nephew, Eumenes I, son of Attalus I. Eumenes had three brothers, and the siblings chose to cooperate with one another rather than fighting among themselves. They ruled successively as the Attalid dynasty, expanding their realm to include the west coast of Anatolia and much of Phrygia, a mountainous region of the interior of modern Turkey. Attalid Greece became known for its fine pottery and tapestries and its ability to compete economically with other Greek successor states. The Attalids traded with Eastern kingdoms, traversing an overland road across Anatolia. They further maintained good relations with Rome, which contributed to their stability and prosperity.

The remaining traditional Greek city states organized into the Aetolian League in the Peloponnesian peninsula or became affiliated with the rival Achaean League. Sparta, Rhodes, and Athens, however, remained somewhat independent after the death of Alexander, although their influence in wider affairs had substantially waned.

The inexorable eastward expansion of its empire brought Rome into contact with the flourishing cities and colonies founded by the Greeks or influenced by Hellenization. First, the Romans reached the city states of Sicily and the Italian mainland, and then in due course their expansion found Hellenistic Greece. Sparta remained independent for a time, but in 195 BC, a coalition of Rome, the Achaean and Aetolian Leagues, Pergamum, and Rhodes defeated the Spartans in the Laconian War. The Spartans were compelled to join the Achaean League, ending the city-state's long tenure as a major power in Greece.

During the next half century, Roman hegemony over the Greek mainland was gradually achieved. In 146 BC, Lucius Mummius Achaicus won a significant military victory over Corinth and the Achaean League. In the aftermath of the Battle of Corinth, the proud city was itself completely destroyed. The ill-advised alliance between Philip V and Hannibal's Carthage contributed mightily to the downfall of

ABOVE: The ruins of the ancient city of Pergamum attract modern visitors. (Creative Commons HALUK COMERTEL via Wikipedia)

Macedonia. About the same time that Corinth met its fate, Macedonia was reduced to the status of the first Roman province in the Aegean world.

To prevent civil war or at least a destructive struggle for power after his death, King Attalus III bequeathed the wealth of Attalid Greece at Pergamum to the Roman republic in his will. When the king died in 133 BC, Roman soldiers marched in to solidify the gain, and the territories of Attalid Greece became the Roman province of Asia, one of the empire's wealthiest.

By 140 BC, decades of infighting had torn the Seleucid empire to tatters. The Romans, however, still considered the Seleucids to be a military threat. Interestingly, it was not until Pompey the Great conquered Seleucid Syria in 66 BC that prospect substantially diminished.

The famous story of Cleopatra VII and her liaisons first with Julius Caesar and then Marc Antony relates the events that brought an end to Ptolemaic Egypt. Although the queen had curried favour for several years, the defeat of Marc Antony's fleet at Actium by the forces of Caesar Augustus (then Octavian) in 31 BC sealed the fate of the last great ruling dynasty in the eastern Mediterranean that could trace its lineage back to Alexander the Great.

Following their conquest of Greece, the Romans bestowed on Athens the status of a free city, most likely due to their great respect for the city as a centre of learning. The Roman admiration for Greek culture is well known, and the Emperor Hadrian visited Athens in 124 AD, returning later to dedicate the great temple of Zeus, whose construction had begun in the 6th century BC. Hadrian became a patron of Athens, authorizing the construction of numerous

buildings and an aqueduct. The citizenry erected a statue in honour of the Roman emperor.

Similarly, the Romans allowed Sparta to continue with its way of life largely undisturbed. In fact, is has been written that wealthy Roman citizens actually travelled to Sparta to observe some of the city's customs, making it an ancient tourist destination of sorts.

Although Greek autonomy had more or less come to an end with Roman rule, Greek influence remained very much alive, shaping Roman culture and civilization, and in a broader context, that of the Western world.

ABOVE: King Philip V of Macedonia formed an alliance with Carthage against Rome during the Second Punic War. (Creative Commons CNG Coins via Wikipedia)

ABOVE: Roman Emperor Hadrian visited Hellenistic Athens and commissioned projects such as this, the Arch of Hadrian, in the city. (Creative Commons A. Savin via Wikipedia)

THE GRACE AND GRANDEUR OF ANCIENT GREECE

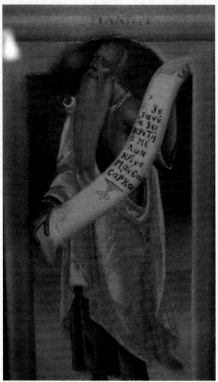

ABOVE: The likeness of Plato is seen in this icon from the early Christian church.
(Creative Commons Nikos D. Karabelis via Wikipedia)

Ancient Greece casts its eminence across nearly three millennia, not in the form of a shadow, but as a great light, a true north of Western civilization. Virtually every aspect of modern living has felt and continues to feel the touch of the ancients whose journey began in a relatively small corner of the eastern Mediterranean world.

Over time, Greek culture spread both east and west, provoking thought, presenting ideas, and offering a wellspring of inspiration from the depth of the human condition to the wonders of the heavens. When the Romans came into contact with Greek civilization, they chose to embrace it, to emulate it so much that some Roman leaders were alarmed. The Roman statesman and philosopher Cicero was among them, and his grandfather, Marcus Tullius Cicero, had said that the better a Roman knew Greek the bigger a rogue he was.

Nevertheless, Cicero had received a Greek education and did acknowledge the significance of it. There was simply no way to deny that the Greeks, slaves that they were, had established a basis for the future appreciation and understanding of broad concepts from human existence to the properties of the physical world. Wealthy Romans sent their children to Greek schools or brought Greek tutors into their homes to teach them. Greek thought, therefore, crept into Roman thought. Greek gods became Roman gods. Greek perspective became Roman perspective. In turn, and through the centuries, then Western perspective lives and has derived its ethos from the cradle of ancient Greece.

Greek philosophers contemplated the world around them, the forces of nature, and the phenomena of the earth, stars and planets. They considered the origins of those energies, seen and unseen. They asked basic questions about the physical world – and deduced answers to some of them. Greek philosophers also turned inward, exploring the realm of the mind. They considered the nature of the individual, the human condition, and the concepts of morality and right and wrong that resonate in Western culture to this day.

It is virtually impossible to learn, comprehend, or discuss the concepts of philosophical exploration without acknowledging the contributions of Socrates, the father of Western thought, Plato, author of the Theory of Forms, and Aristotle, the philosopher and scientist who delved into so many aspects of mankind's existence, the animal kingdom, and more. What is truth? What is beauty? What does it mean to live a virtuous life? If those who study the great philosophers of ancient Greece do not find answers, they at least discover points of view, offered by some of the greatest intellectuals of all time.

Ancient Greece brought the foundations of Western thought and ideas from the realm of the theoretical into the practical as well. The theatre was born in Ancient Greece, and from it we have inherited the performing arts. Drama, music, and motion pictures find their lineage in the manuscripts of antiquity that survive in full or in fragments. Tragedy and comedy, the sorrow and laughter, and the gamut of human emotion are conveyed today on the evolutionary shoulders of

ABOVE: Archimedes was a towering figure among mathematicians in ancient Greece. (Public Domain)

ABOVE: The ascetic Diogenes, lamp in hand, searches for an 'honest man.' (Public Domain)

ABOVE: Troy is seen in flames as the city is sacked and burned by Greek soldiers. (Creative Commons Jl FilpoC via Wikipedia)

theorems and formulas that facilitated investigation and invention. Medicine found its footing and charted the course toward modern times, and today's doctors pay homage to the great Greek physician with the Hippocratic Oath, its earliest pledge reading, "I swear by Apollo healer, by Asclepius, by Hygieia, by Panacea, and by all the gods and goddesses, making them my witnesses, that I will carry out, according to my ability and judgment, this oath and this indenture."

In real perspective, it must be noted that the ancient Greeks were not without those flaws that plague human existence. There were those among them whose lust for power, wealth, and affluence led to jealousy, mistrust, militarism, conquest, gain and loss. They made war against outside empires and principalities as well as within, and in doing so hastening the demise of their own power and prestige. But those who stood at Marathon, the brave 300 at Thermopylae, and the stalwarts of Salamis secured their places in history, defending their own culture and proving themselves stewards of generations yet to come as they preserved Western culture.

The military conquests of Alexander the Great inspire awe, while the associated ruthlessness and expansionism have offered warnings for the future. In Alexander's wake, the absence of a worthy successor led to the epic rivalry for the spoils of war and the eventual rise and fall of his one-time lieutenants. Therein, perhaps, lies another lesson, one of strength in unity.

The panorama of ancient Greece unfolds for the modern reader and lover of history like a fantastic tapestry. Heroes and heroines, gods and men, the eminent and the ordinary, all played roles in an era that spanned the centuries of old to inspire, empower, and uplift those who followed. The inheritors of the legacy of ancient Greece find the common thread that binds them to their ancestors almost everywhere – in their language, their entertainment, their educational institutions, their buildings and their beliefs.

The story of ancient Greece, therefore, is not over. It continues as long as Western civilization and culture exist. And the real relevance of any story remains most vigorously tantalizing with the prospect of that which remains unfinished.

ABOVE: The Greek philosopher and scientist Aristotle is shown at his writing desk in this 15th century illustration. (Public Domain)

ancient masters such as Aeschylus, Sophocles, Aristophanes, Euripides, and others.

The architecture of ancient Greece is reflected in the soaring temples, great amphitheatres, and magnificent symmetry envisioned and constructed by its creators. For example, even in ruin, the Parthenon has stood the test of time representative of incredible form and grace. The term "Greek Revival" is proof enough that architecture, conceived in the classical lines and contours of ancient world, will endure. It is seen among the many great modern buildings and public structures and spaces that are revered across the globe.

The concept of democracy, representative government wherein the political authority derives its capacity to govern from the people,

has survived and flourished, energizing movements in Europe and North America more than two millennia after its first stirrings in ancient Athens. The method and the maintenance of it have evolved, and it exists today in various degrees and interpretations. But without the conscious efforts of Solon, Cleisthenes and others, would the spark of representative democracy have ever become a flame? For all its imperfection, democracy has matured into a political public policy in which some live today and a circumstance that others continue to seek.

The genius of ancient Greece has left its legacy in the body of knowledge and the applications produced in research, experimentation, and logical deduction. Plotting the movements of the moon and stars, explaining the transits of celestial bodies that produce a lunar or solar eclipse, and theorizing the positions of the earth and the sun in the cosmos fascinate us to this day. And the remarkable conclusions proven by ancient Greek astronomers provided the foundation of future discovery.

At the same time, mathematicians altered accepted views of the world with

ABOVE: This painting of the Temple of Hephaestus depicts an excellent example of ancient Greek architecture. (Public Domain)

GLIMPSES OF ANCIENT GREECE

The glory that was Ancient Greece remains today. Its timeless tales of gods and heroes, beauty and majesty resonate across the centuries along with the stories of war and peace, internal and external strife, myth and legend. The birth of democracy and the soaring grandeur of the Parthenon in Athens, the incredible heroism of 300 men at Thermopylae, and the wisdom of Socrates are only the beginning. The Ancient Greek civilization established the framework of Western culture, and the influence of its philosophers, poets, playwrights, artists, scientists, and warriors is found in virtually every aspect of modern living. Experience the adventure. Find the common thread. Expand historical horizons. And enjoy these pages created in homage to the ancients. This journey through time is a voyage of discovery and appreciation for the achievements of those who lived more than two millennia ago.

BELOW: Ancient Greek musicians and worshippers celebrate the sunrise in this 19th century painting. (Public Domain)